**Mel Bay presents**

# 101 Essential Country Chord Progressions

**Chord Diagrams Included • For All Musicians and Song Writers**

*by Larry McCabe*

## CD CONTENTS

| | | | | | |
|---|---|---|---|---|---|
| 1 "A" tuning note | 18 Ex. 17 | 35 Ex. 34 | 52 Ex. 51 | 69 Ex. 68 | 86 Ex. 85 |
| 2 Ex. 1 | 19 Ex. 18 | 36 Ex. 35 | 53 Ex. 52 | 70 Ex. 69 | 87 Ex. 86 |
| 3 Ex. 2 | 20 Ex. 19 | 37 Ex. 36 | 54 Ex. 53 | 71 Ex. 70 | 88 Ex. 87-88 |
| 4 Ex. 3 | 21 Ex. 20 | 38 Ex. 37 | 55 Ex. 54 | 72 Ex. 71 | 89 Ex. 89-90 |
| 5 Ex. 4 | 22 Ex. 21 | 39 Ex. 38 | 56 Ex. 55 | 73 Ex. 72 | 90 Ex. 91-92 |
| 6 Ex. 5 | 23 Ex. 22 | 40 Ex. 39 | 57 Ex. 56 | 74 Ex. 73 | 91 Ex. 93 |
| 7 Ex. 6 | 24 Ex. 23 | 41 Ex. 40 | 58 Ex. 57 | 75 Ex. 74 | 92 Ex. 94 |
| 8 Ex. 7 | 25 Ex. 24 | 42 Ex. 41 | 59 Ex. 58 | 76 Ex. 75 | 93 Ex. 95 |
| 9 Ex. 8 | 26 Ex. 25 | 43 Ex. 42 | 60 Ex. 59 | 77 Ex. 76 | 94 Ex. 96 |
| 10 Ex. 9 | 27 Ex. 26 | 44 Ex. 43 | 61 Ex. 60 | 78 Ex. 77 | 95 Ex. 97 |
| 11 Ex. 10 | 28 Ex. 27 | 45 Ex. 44 | 62 Ex. 61 | 79 Ex. 78 | 96 Ex. 98 |
| 12 Ex. 11 | 29 Ex. 28 | 46 Ex. 45 | 63 Ex. 62 | 80 Ex. 79 | 97 Ex. 99 |
| 13 Ex. 12 | 30 Ex. 29 | 47 Ex. 46 | 64 Ex. 63 | 81 Ex. 80 | 98 Ex. 100 |
| 14 Ex. 13 | 31 Ex. 30 | 48 Ex. 47 | 65 Ex. 64 | 82 Ex. 81 | 99 Ex. 101 |
| 15 Ex. 14 | 32 Ex. 31 | 49 Ex. 48 | 66 Ex. 65 | 83 Ex. 82 | |
| 16 Ex. 15 | 33 Ex. 32 | 50 Ex. 49 | 67 Ex. 66 | 84 Ex. 83 | |
| 17 Ex. 16 | 34 Ex. 33 | 51 Ex. 50 | 68 Ex. 67 | 85 Ex. 84 | |

## CONTENTS

| | |
|---|---|
| Introduction | 2 |
| Projects for Students, Musicians and Writers | 2 |
| How to Use This Book | 3 |
| COUNTRY CHORD PROGRESSIONS IN MAJOR KEYS | 5 |
|    4-Bar Progressions (Ex. 1-50 in 4/4; Ex. 51-60 in 3/4) | 20 |
|    8-Bar Progressions (Ex. 61-64) | 22 |
|    16-Bar Progressions (Ex. 65-69) | 27 |
|    16-Bar Verse/Chorus Progressions (Ex. 70-73) | 31 |
|    32-Bar Verse/Chorus Progressions (Ex. 74-75) | 35 |
|    12-Bar Blues Progression (Ex. 76) | 36 |
|    32-Bar AABA Progressions (Ex. 77-78) | 40 |
|    8-Bar Bridge Progressions (Ex. 79-86) | 44 |
|    Turnarounds (Ex. 87-90) | |
| COUNTRY CHORD PROGRESSIONS IN MINOR KEYS | 45 |
|    4-Bar Progressions (ex. 91-99) | 48 |
|    8-Bar Progressions (ex. 100-101) | |

1 2 3 4 5 6 7 8 9 0

© 2002 BY MEL BAY PUBLICATIONS, INC., PACIFIC, MO 63069.
ALL RIGHTS RESERVED. INTERNATIONAL COPYRIGHT SECURED. B.M.I. MADE AND PRINTED IN U.S.A.
No part of this publication may be reproduced in whole or in part, or stored in a retrieval system, or transmitted in any form
or by any means, electronic, mechanical, photocopy, recording, or otherwise, without written permission of the publisher.

Visit us on the Web at www.melbay.com — E-mail us at email@melbay.com

# INTRODUCTION

On the surface, today's "Nashville Sound" bears little resemblance to the "hillbilly" country music of the past. Nowadays, when the recording artist arrives at the 64-track digital recording session, his legal advisor is jabbering into a cell phone, his public relations counselor is waiting in the stretch limo outside, and his trendy hairstylist is on 24-hour call. Perfectly understandable. You never know when there will be a cosmetic emergency–or another unendurable crisis of the moment.

Back in grandpa's time, the bib overall-attired recording star required only his frailing banjo, a packet of chewing tobacco, and maybe a crock of corn liquor for inspiration and stamina. Of course, if he was versatile he might have a Marine Band harmonica stashed in the bibs for train whistles and bird calls. Beyond that, he had no amplifier, no agent . . . zilch.

However, appearances can be misleading: if we compare the chords played in new country songs to the chords heard in the old tunes, we see (and hear) that little has changed. With this in mind, this book of *101 Essential Country Chord Progressions* was designed to help you play and write songs in both contemporary and classic country styles. Whether you prefer your country traditional, modern, or inbetween, these chord progressions will help spice up your playing, singing, and song writing.

We're including a CD so that you can hear every chord progression in the book. Regretfully, we must ask you to pick up your own tab for the recording session, the limousine, and the optional overalls.

Larry McCabe
Tallahassee, Florida

## Credits

Randy Barnhill, bass; Larry McCabe, guitar; Leon Roberts, steel guitar; Fred Chester, engineer.

If you enjoy this book, please see the Mel Bay catalog, or visit melbay.com, to review additional Mel Bay titles by Larry McCabe.

## Procedure

Because this book is not a graded method, you can work through the examples in any order. Beginning instrumentalists may wish to start with the 4-bar and turnaround progressions.

# PROJECTS FOR STUDENTS, MUSICIANS, & WRITERS

This book is designed to serve a wide range of individual needs. The following projects will benefit all musicians and writers. Teachers can assign the projects as needed.

1. Transpose each chord progression to several other keys.

2. Write out the *formula* (scale tones from which the chord is derived) for each chord in a progression. For example, the formula for a dominant chord (C7, F7, G7, etc.) is 1-3-5-♭7, meaning the first, third, fifth, and flatted seventh tones of the C scale.

3. Write out the spelling for each chord. The term *chord spelling* simply means the notes of the chord; for example, the spelling for C7 is C E G B♭.

4. Apply each formula (and transpose each spelling) to all root tones. If you need help with chord theory, formulas and spellings, see *Complete Book of Guitar Chords, Scales and Arpeggios* (94792).

5. Create several original songs by combining or modifying progressions from the book.

6. Keyboard players should write out logical chord voicings for the chord changes.

7. Try to learn several progressions by ear from the companion CD.

8. Instrumentalists: jam or compose original solos, phrases, or bass lines to the chord progressions.

9. Songwriters and composers: write original lyrics and music to the chord progressions.

10. Recording studios and arrangers can write or play "instant" original songs and arrangements to the chord progressions.

11. Advertising agencies can refer to the chord progressions as ideas for quick background ideas.

If any of these concepts are unclear, see a good music teacher for guidance.

# HOW TO USE THIS BOOK

This book is for music students, teachers, performing artists, recording studios, composers, songwriters, advertising agencies, and any person or music company who desires a user-friendly, comprehensive guide to country chord progressions. All creative musicians and writers who study, perform, or compose country music will benefit from this book. In addition, the companion CD is ideal for jamming and ear training.

The chord progressions in this book can be used for performing, composing, and studying all country styles including contemporary, classic honky-tonk, bluegrass, gospel, old-time, country rock, Western swing, fiddle tunes, country blues, and folk music. For your convenience, blank music staff paper is provided for composing lyrics, melodies, bass lines, chord voicings, licks, and solos.

Every progression in the book is in the key of C major or its relative minor key, A minor. This format provides a consistent point of reference while facilitating ease in analyzing and comparing examples.

## The Chord Charts

Each chord progression is presented in the form of a chord chart which is designed as follows:

    a) Chord names are supplied above each measure.
    b) Chord frames (specific voicings) are supplied for guitarists.
    c) Blank staves for both treble and bass clefs can serve as worksheets for study or composition.
    d) Each chart represents either a section of a chord progression, or an entire chord progression.

The various types of progressions taught in this book are explained below.

## Chord Symbols

Chord frames are included for guitar players. Keyboard players and others should have no trouble creating chord voicings from the chord symbols.

## Song Forms and Chord Progressions

### Standard Song Forms and Phrases

Four basic song forms are used extensively in country and folk music. All of these standard song forms, along with typical chord phrases, are covered in this book.

1. An **AAA song** is a song with verses only. In country music, the verses for AAA songs can be 8 bars or–more commonly–16 bars in length. Some country verses are 32 bars long ("Knoxville Girl").

2. An **AB** song is also known as a **verse-chorus** song. Often, the country/folk AB song has a 16-bar verse and a 16-bar chorus; however, each section could also be 8, 12, 16, 20, 24, or 32 bars long.

3. A **12-bar blues progression** contains three 4-bar phrases known as AAB: the melody is played or sung over four bars (A), another four-bar A phrase follows, and a concluding B section (a contrasting melody) completes the progression:

    (A) Wonder why my bulldog bites so hard,
    (A) Wonder why my bulldog bites so hard,
    (B) Mailman left his big toe in my yard.

4. A **32-bar AABA song** has four sections: The *A section* (also called the *opening section*) is played once and repeated. A contrasting section–known as the *bridge* –then follows the repeated A section. The bridge is also called the *B section*. Sometimes the bridge is played in a different key than the A section. Collectively, the combining of the four sections is called *AABA*. In country songs, each section of an AABA song is usually eight measures in length, producing a *32-bar AABA*.

### Progressions Covered in This Book

• The **4-bar progressions** (Ex. 1-60 major; Ex. 91-99 minor) are typical harmonic phrases found in many songs. In the major keys, examples 1-50 are in 4/4 (common) time while examples 51-60 are in 3/4 (waltz) time. The minor-key examples (Ex. 91-99) are in 4/4 time; however, as with the other progressions in this book, many of the 4/4 examples could be converted to 3/4, and vice-versa.

Suggested uses: 1) Join two 4-bar progressions together to create an eight-bar verse or chorus; 2) Join two 4-bar progressions together to create either an A section or a B section for a 32-bar AABA song (see below); 3) Join four 4-bar progressions together to create a 16-bar verse or chorus, etc. It is possible to mix major and relative minor progressions to create new progressions.

• An **8-bar progression** (Ex. 61-64 major; Ex. 100-101 minor) can be used in any of the following ways: 1) A verse of an 8-bar AAA (verses-only) song; 2) The verse and/or chorus progression of a 16-bar verse-chorus song; or 3) The A section of a 32-bar AABA song.

• A **16-bar progression** (Ex. 65-69) could represent any of the following: 1) A verse of a 16-bar AAA song (verses only); 2) The verse and/or chorus progression of a 32-bar verse-chorus song.

• A **16-bar verse/chorus progression** (Ex. 70-73) is an AB progression containing an 8-bar verse followed by an 8-bar chorus. In applying these progressions, it is possible to play more than one verse before playing the chorus. Another possibility: begin with the chorus.

• The **32-bar verse/chorus progressions** (Ex. 74-75) are extended versions of the 16-bar verse/chorus progressions discussed above.

• The **12-bar blues progression** (Ex. 76) in this book represents a typical three-chord country blues progression ("Corrine, Corrina"). Jimmie Rodgers, the "Father of Country Music," was actually more of a blues singer than a pure country musician. Early jazz musicians such as Louis Armstrong (who recorded with Rodgers for RCA), while adhering to the 12-bar form, added more chords to bring the blues to a higher level of harmonic sophistication in the 1920s. However, most country musicians still use only three chords when playing the blues.

• The **32-bar AABA progression** (Ex. 77-78) is discussed above. Well-known AABA country songs include "Walking After Midnight," "I Fall to Pieces," "End of the World."

• An **8-bar bridge progression** (Ex. 79-86) is the B section in an AABA progression. Project: Create a major-key AABA progression by matching an 8-bar progression (Ex. 61-64) with a complimentary bridge section (Ex. 79-86). The "8-bar progression" will be used for the A sections; the "8-bar bridge" will be the B section. Feel free to change chords here and there to make the parts fit together logically.

• A **turnaround** (Ex. 87-90) is a two-bar harmonic phrase found at the end of a chord progression or section of music. For example, a turnaround could be played in measures 7-8 of an 8-bar verse, or in measures 11-12 of a 12-bar blues. A turnaround could also be played in the last two bars of either an A section or a B section.

## The Companion CD

1. An extended "A" tuning beep is provided on the first track of the companion CD.

2. The CD, recorded in stereo, is mixed as follows: The drums and rhythm guitar are in the center
   The pedal steel guitar is on the right
   The bass is on the left

3. If you wish, you can remove either the pedal steel guitar or the bass by turning down the appropriate speaker.

4. Because the current technology permits only 99 tracks, it was necessary to double a few examples on the CD.

5. The background is kept very simple to minimize clashing with your original ideas.

## Procedure

Because this book is not a graded method, you can work through the examples in any order. Beginning instrumentalists may wish to start with the 4-bar and turnaround progressions.

# Four-Bar Chord Progressions

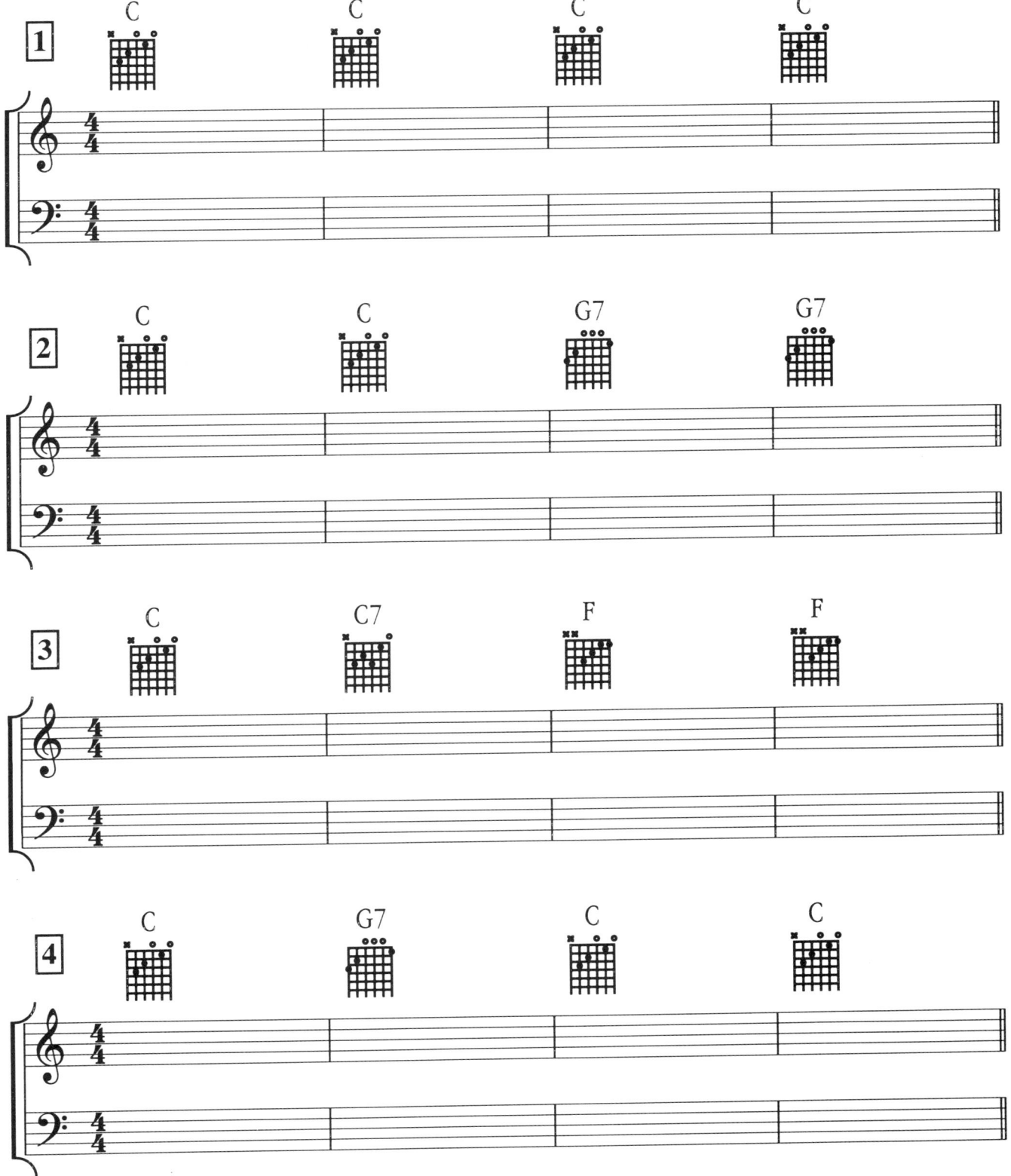

## Four-Bar Chord Progressions . . . continued

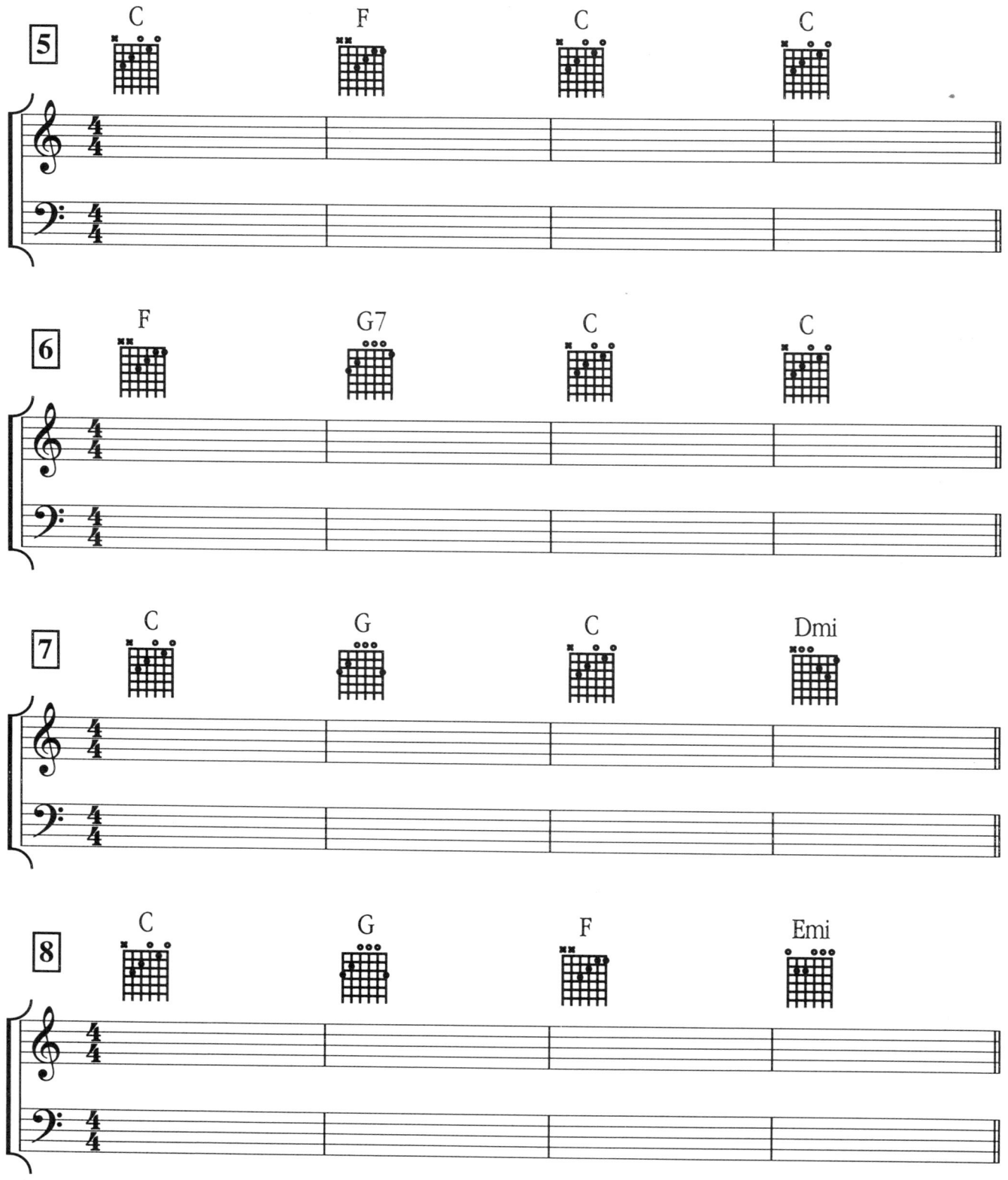

## Four-Bar Chord Progressions . . . continued

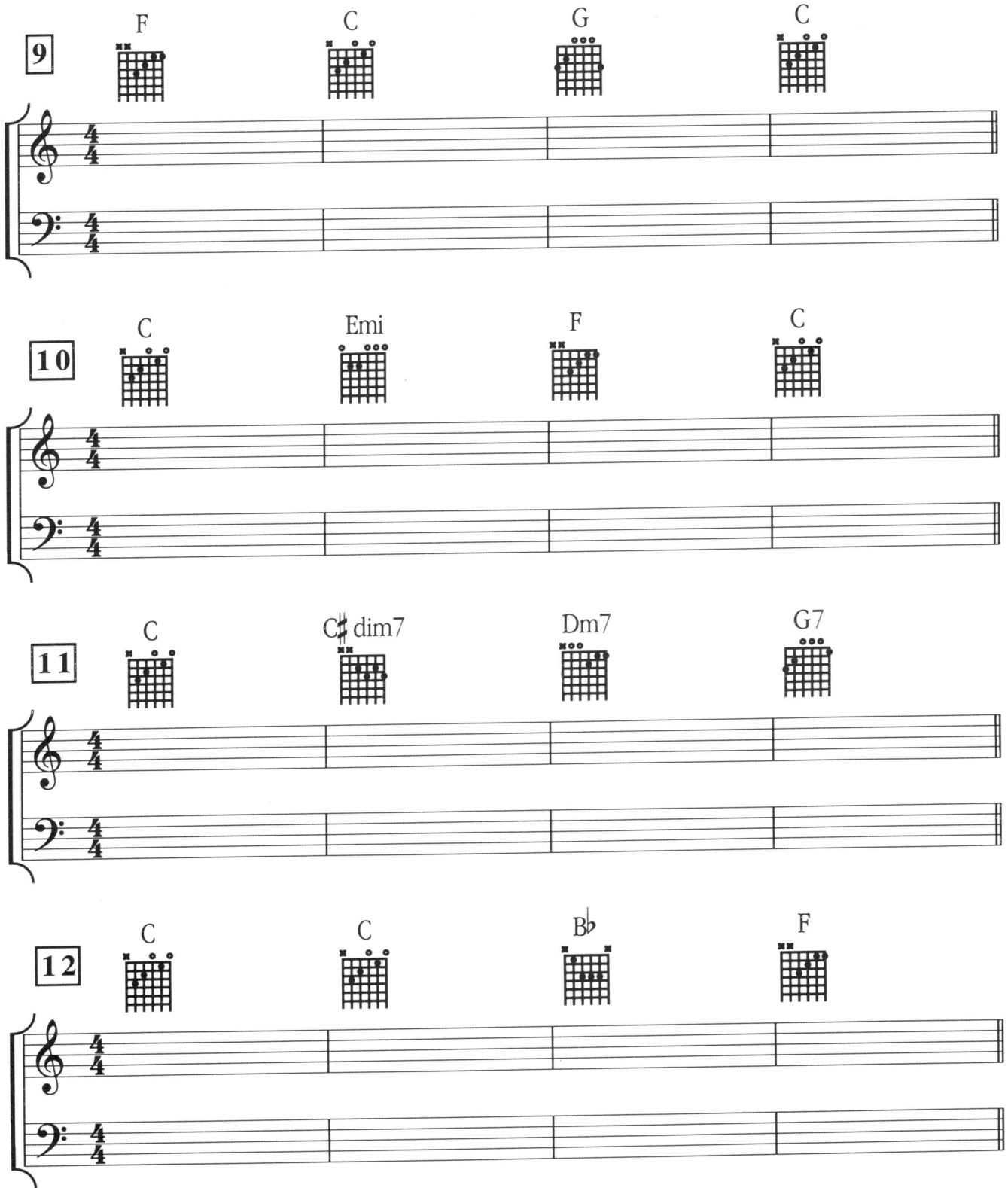

## Four-Bar Chord Progressions . . . continued

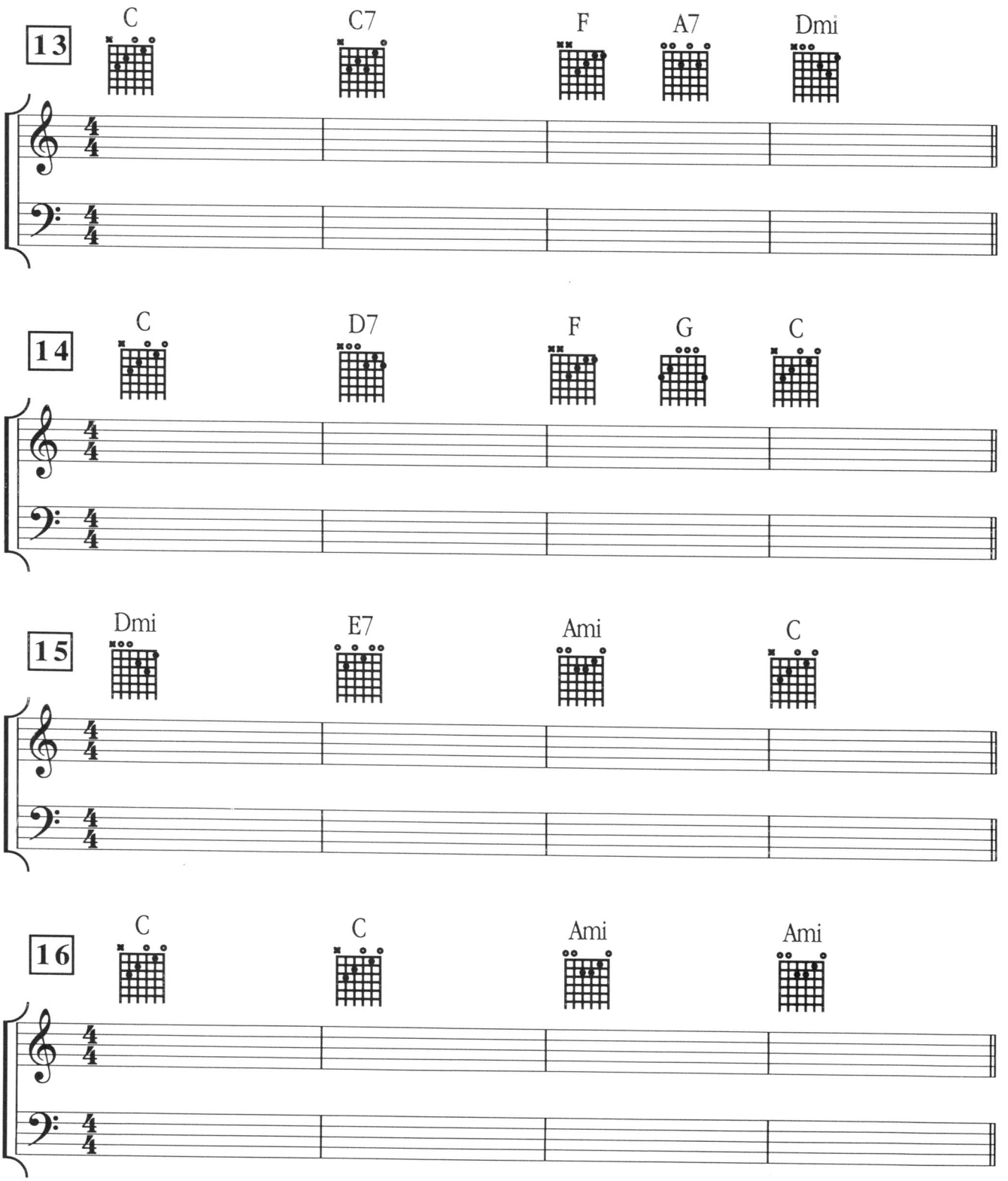

## Four-Bar Chord Progressions . . . continued

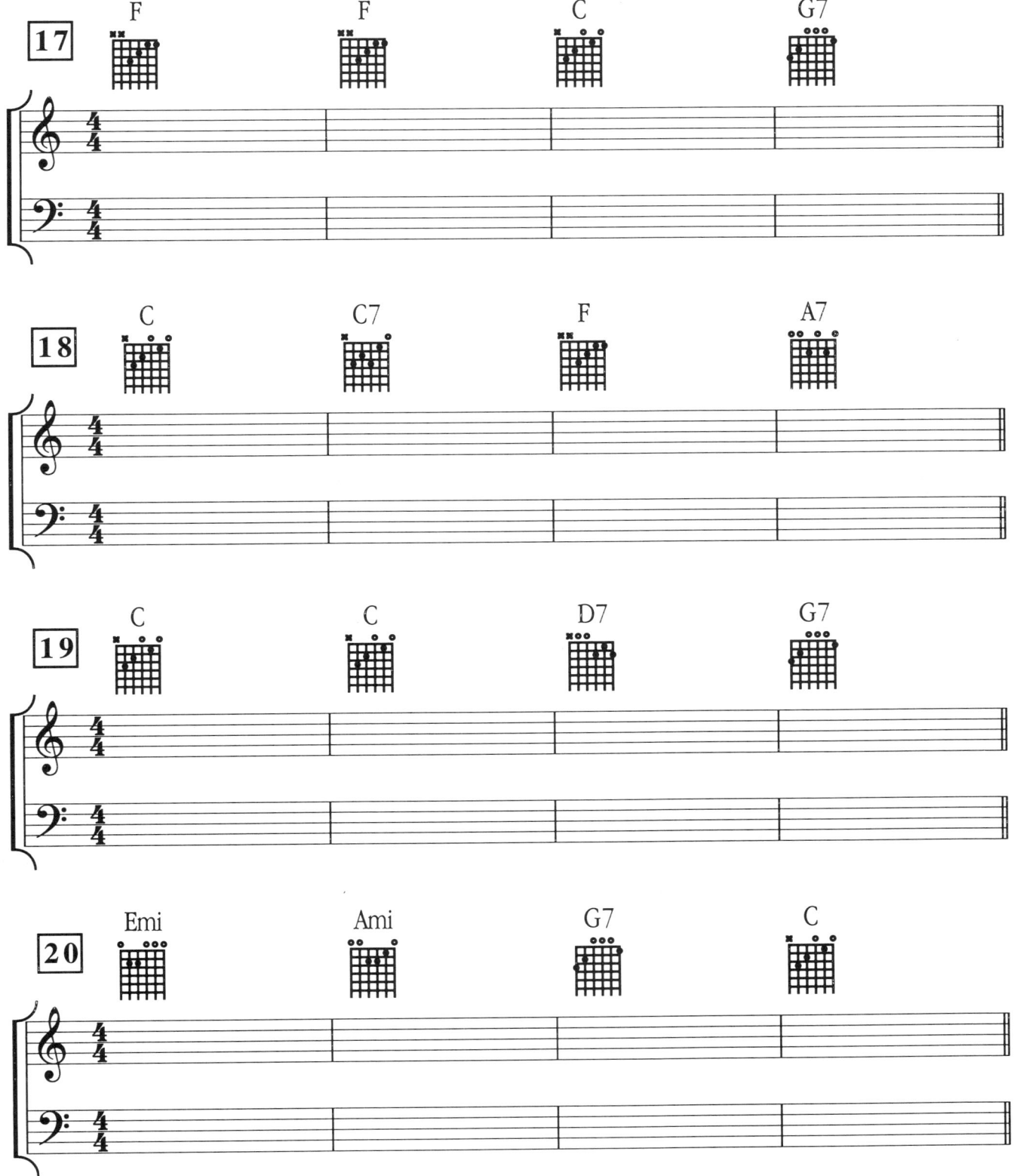

## Four-Bar Chord Progressions . . . continued

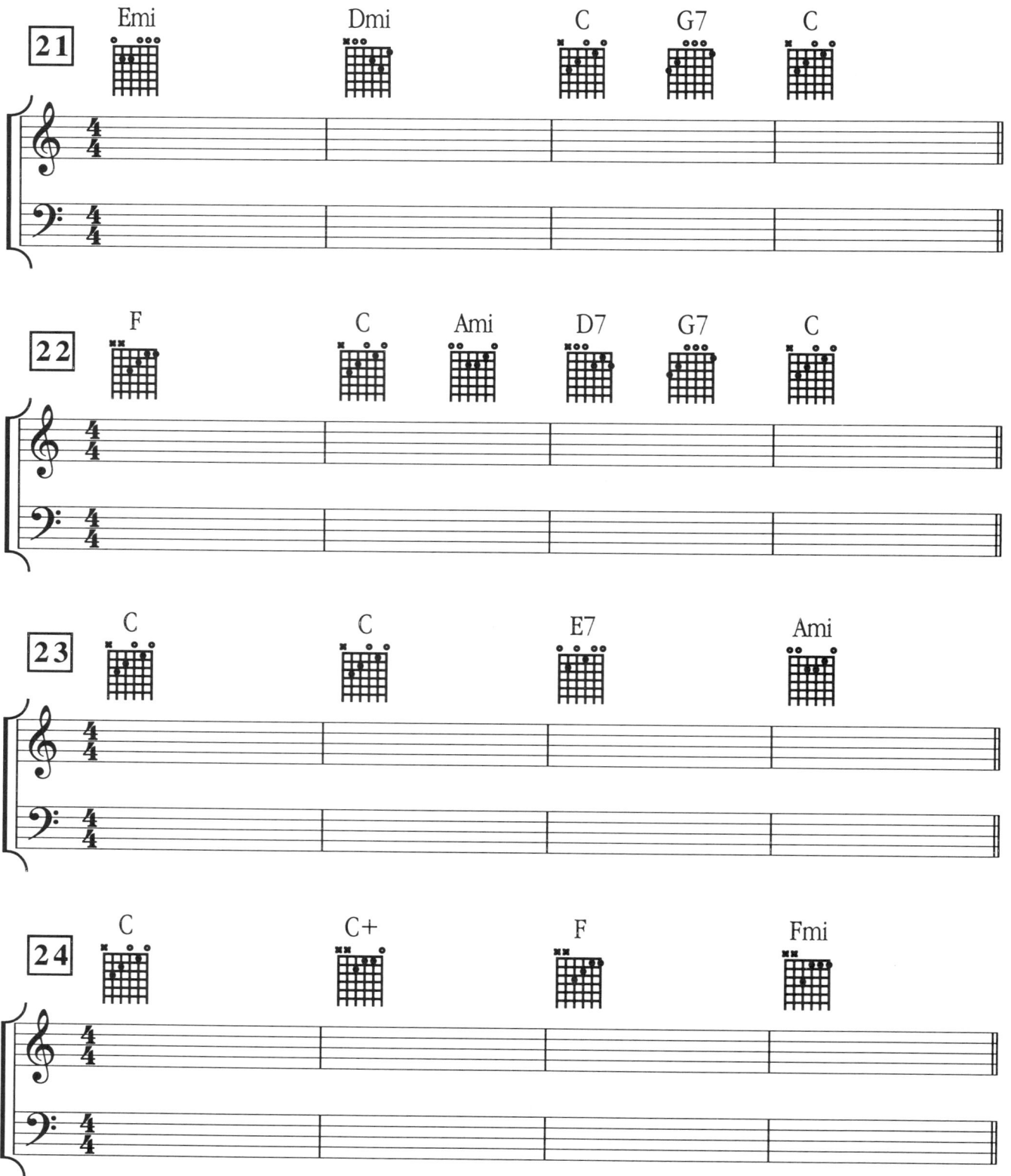

## Four-Bar Chord Progressions . . . continued

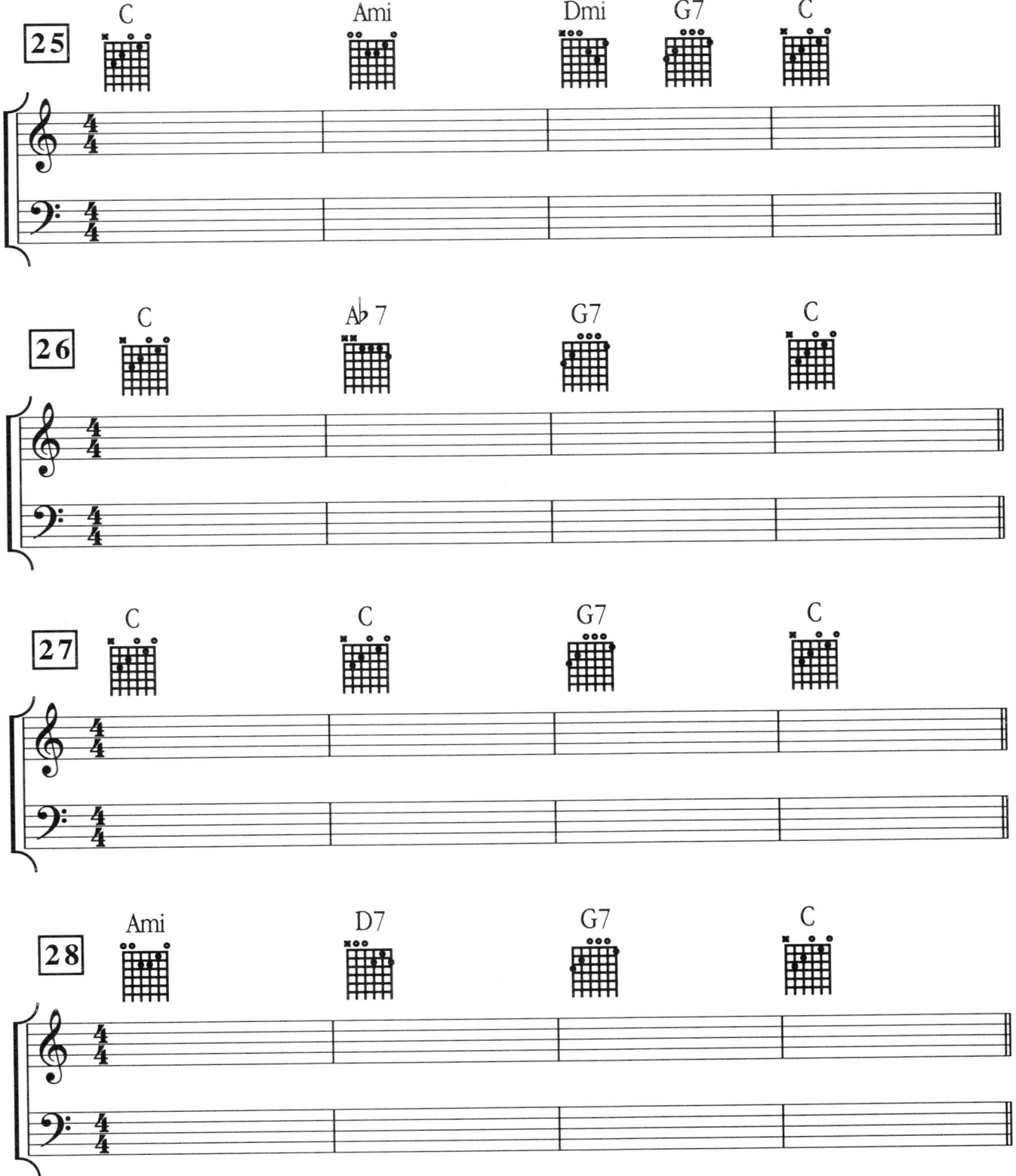

## Four-Bar Chord Progressions . . . continued

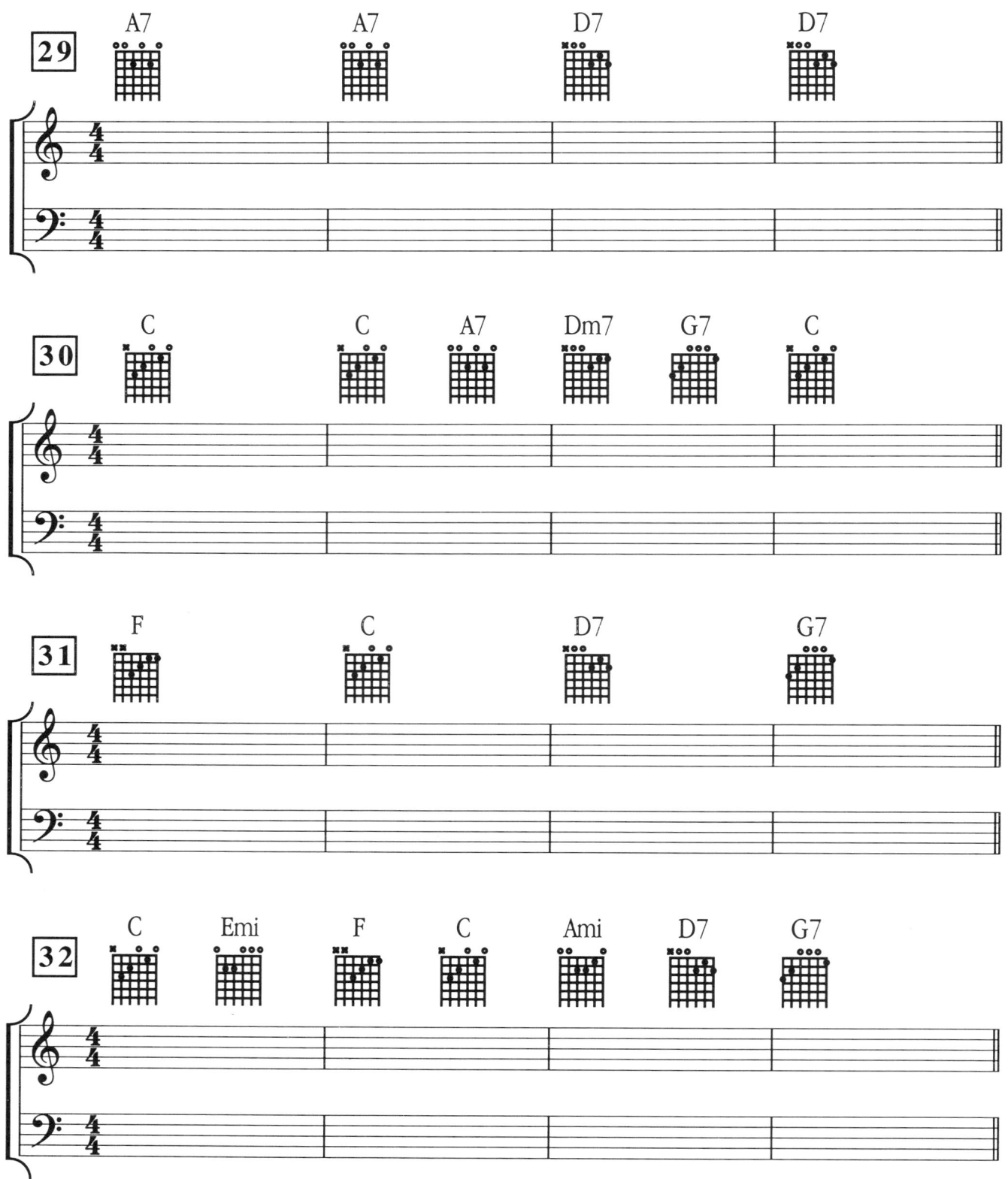

## Four-Bar Chord Progressions . . . continued

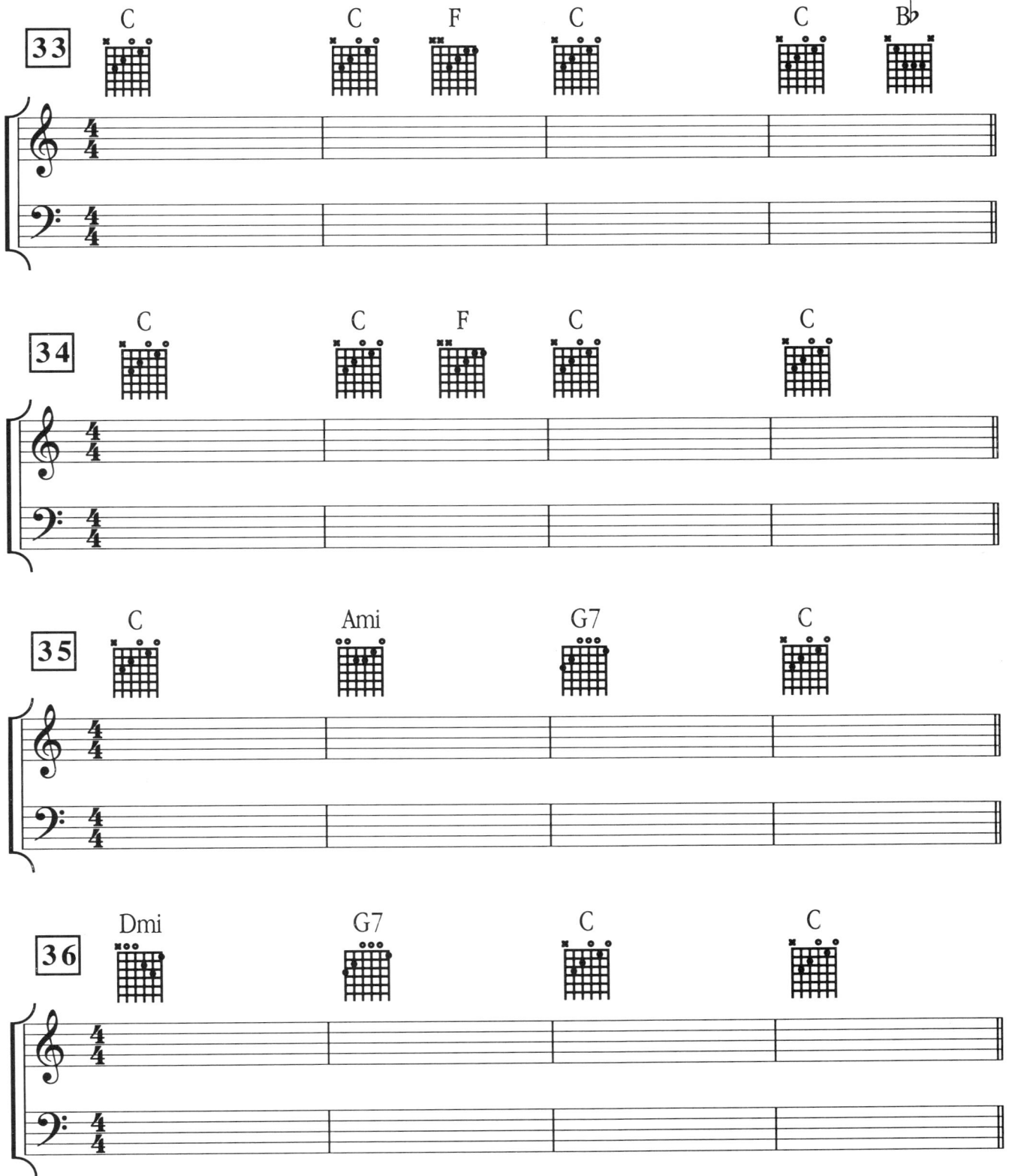

## Four-Bar Chord Progressions . . . continued

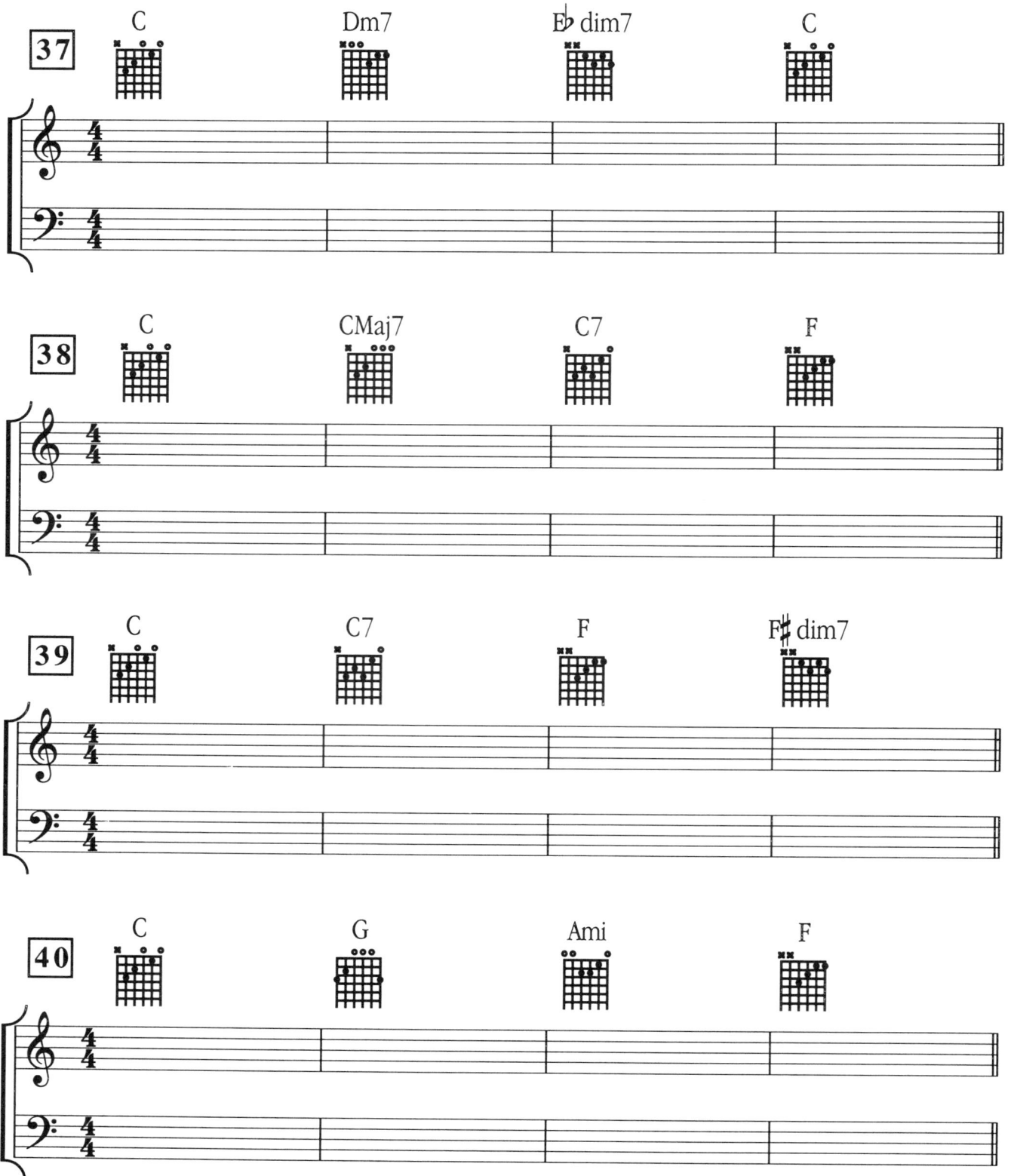

## Four-Bar Chord Progressions . . . continued

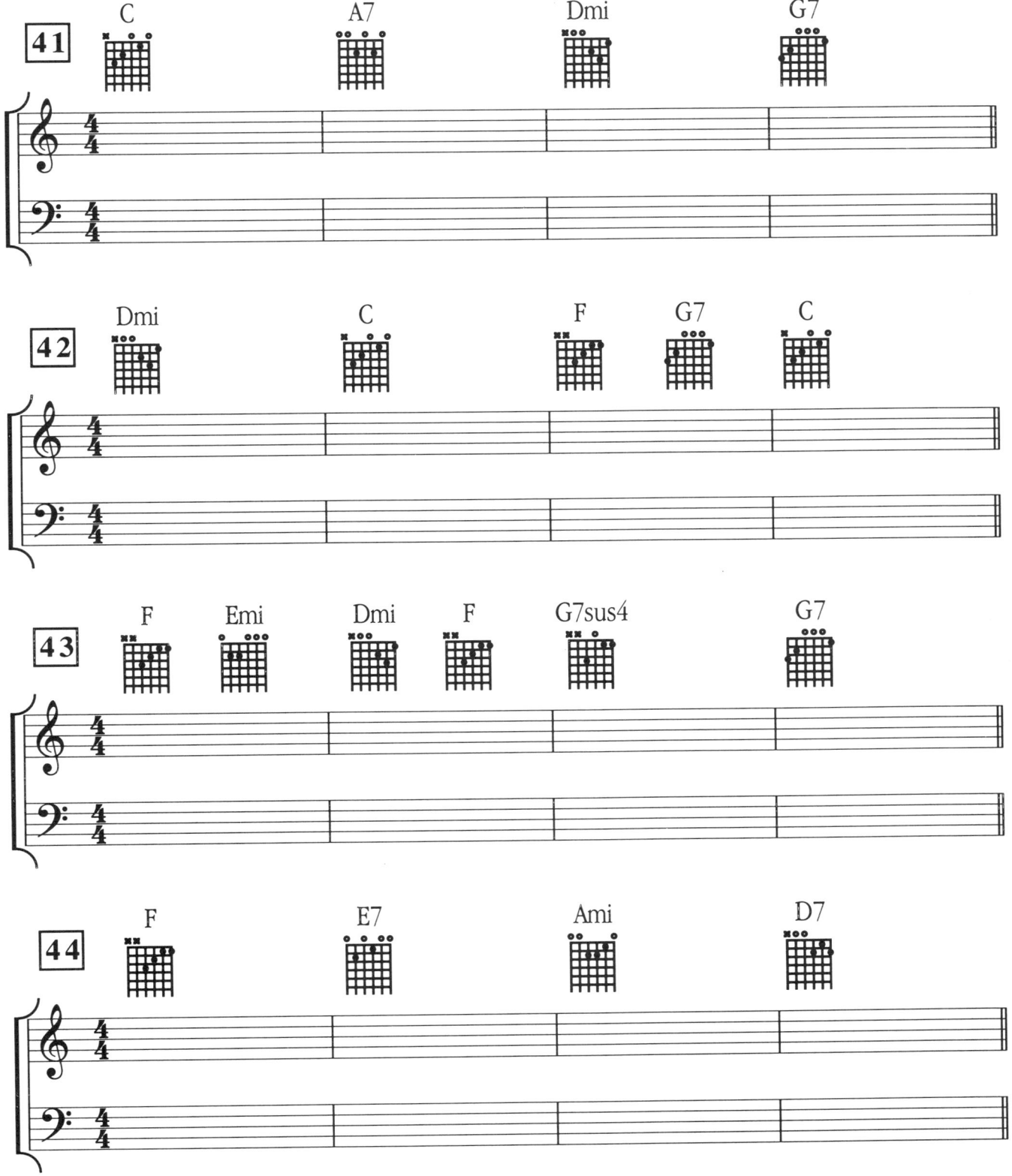

# Four-Bar Chord Progressions . . . continued

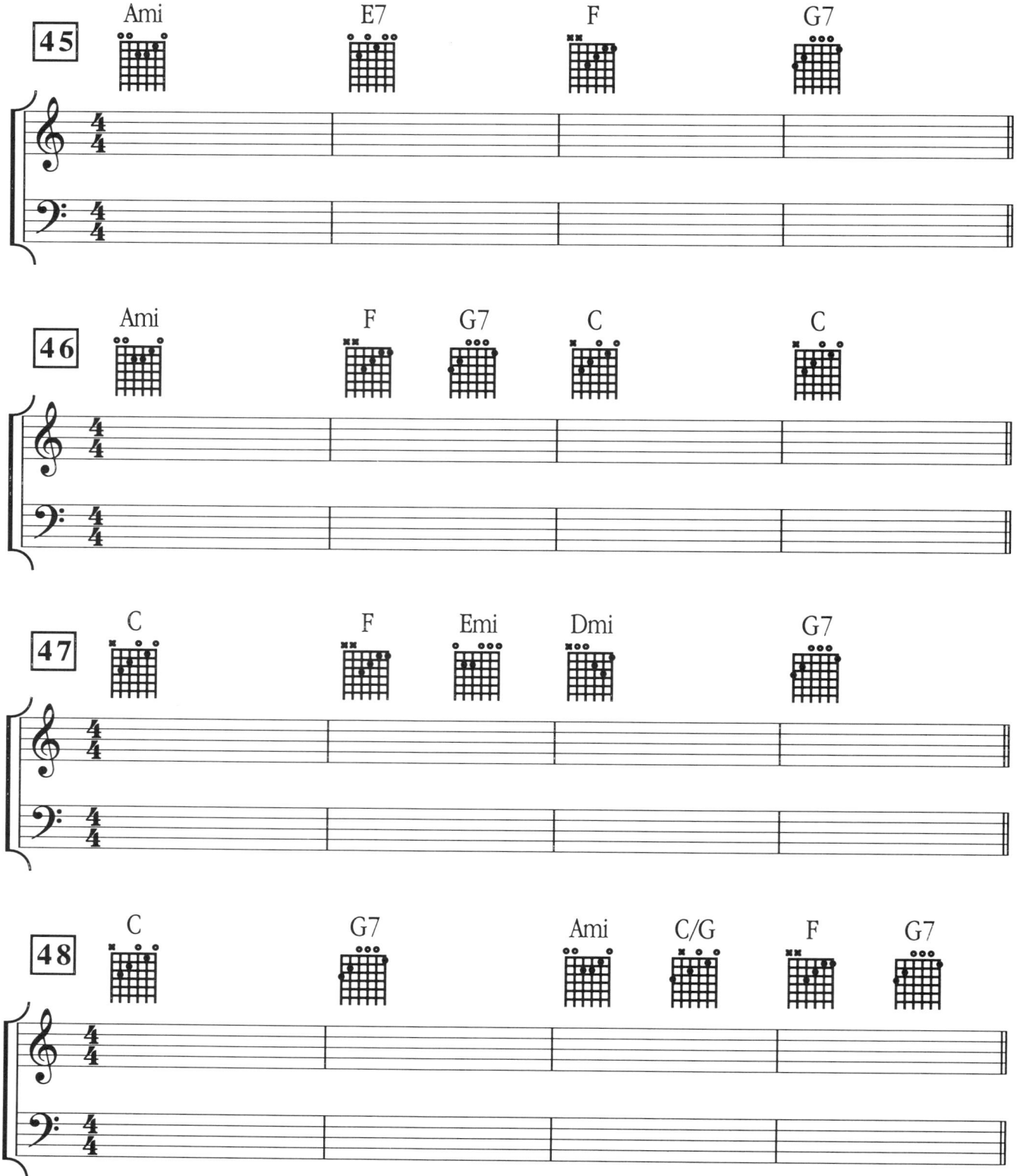

# Four-Bar Chord Progressions . . . continued

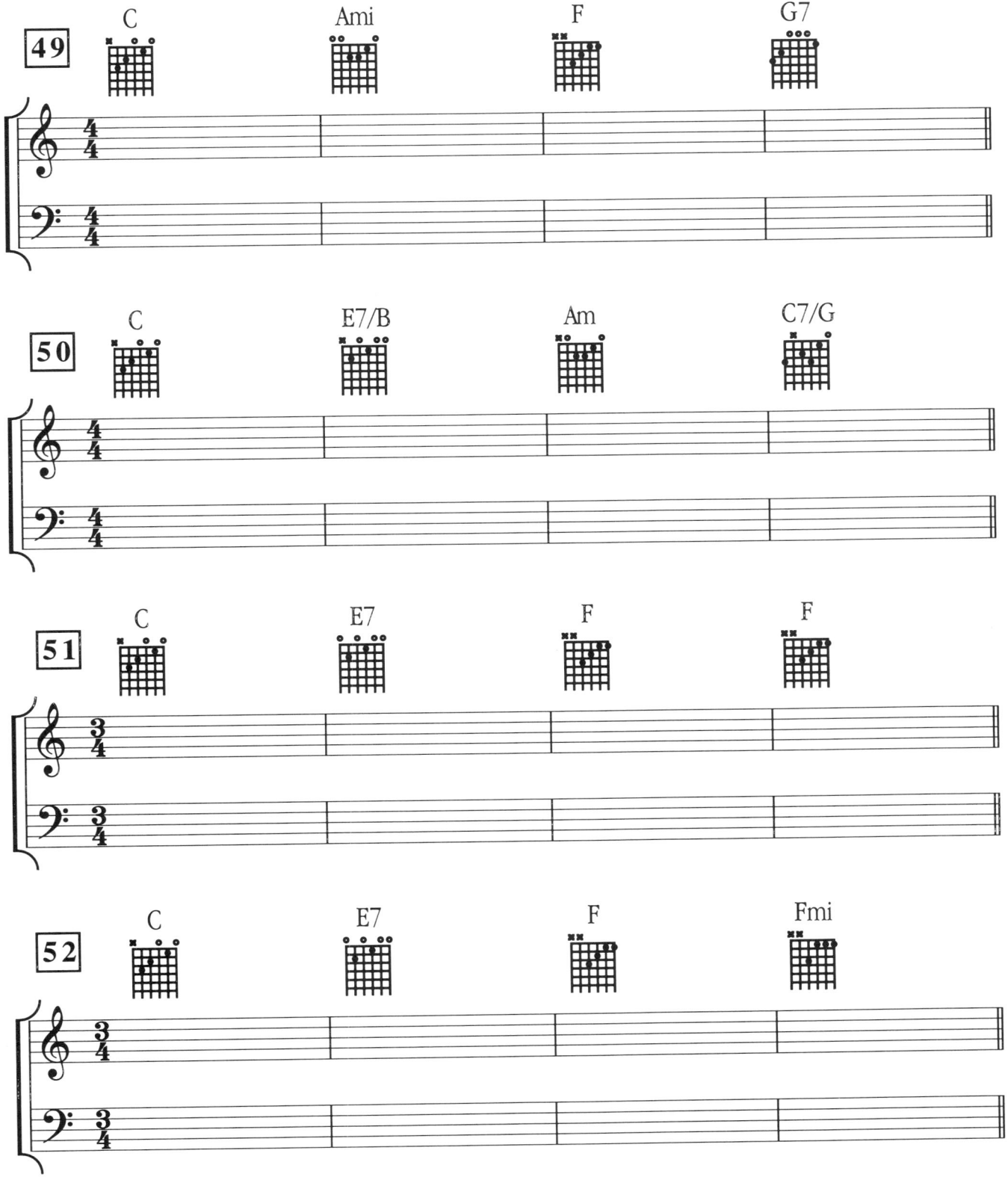

## Four-Bar Chord Progressions . . . continued

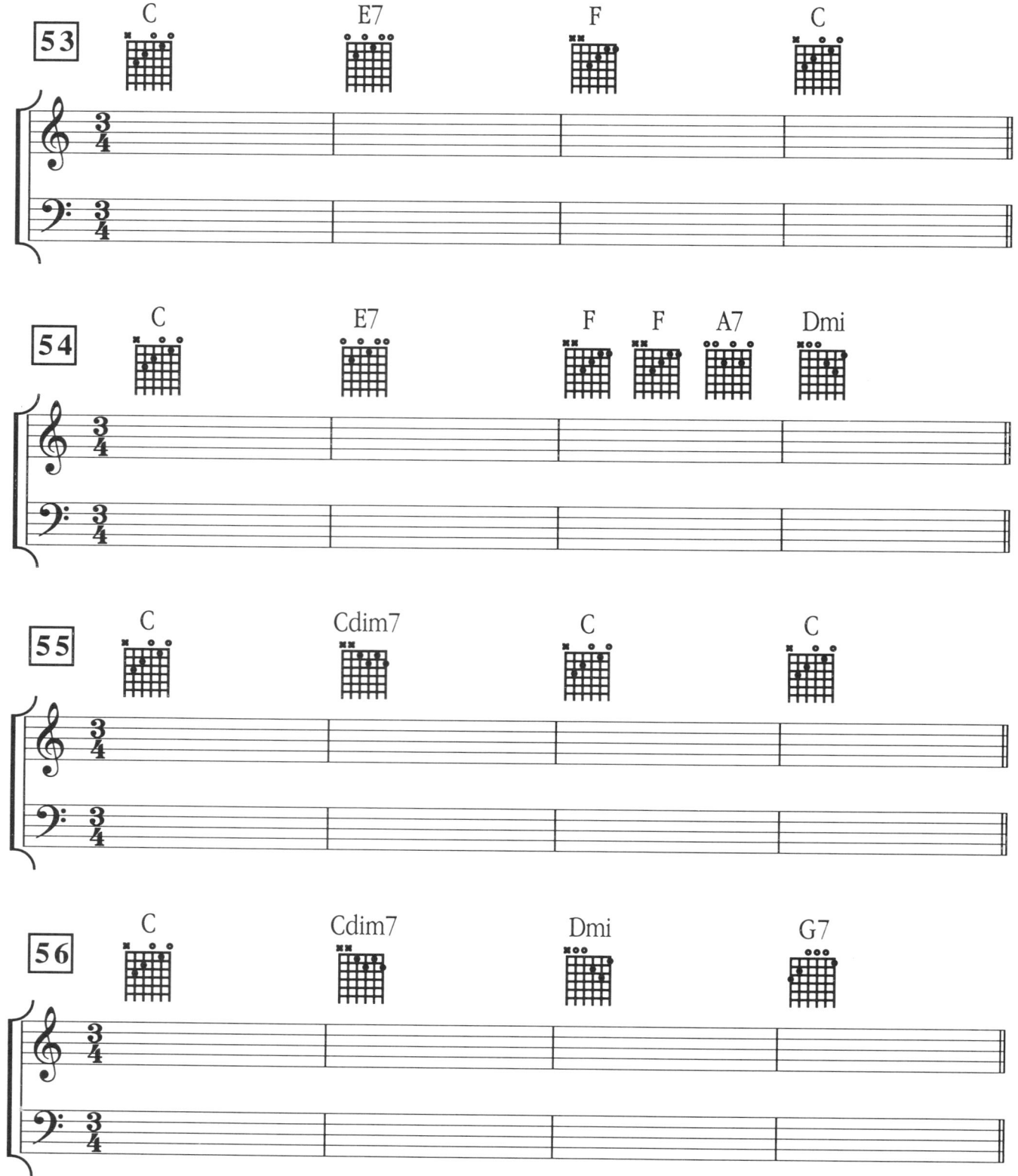

## Four-Bar Chord Progressions ... continued

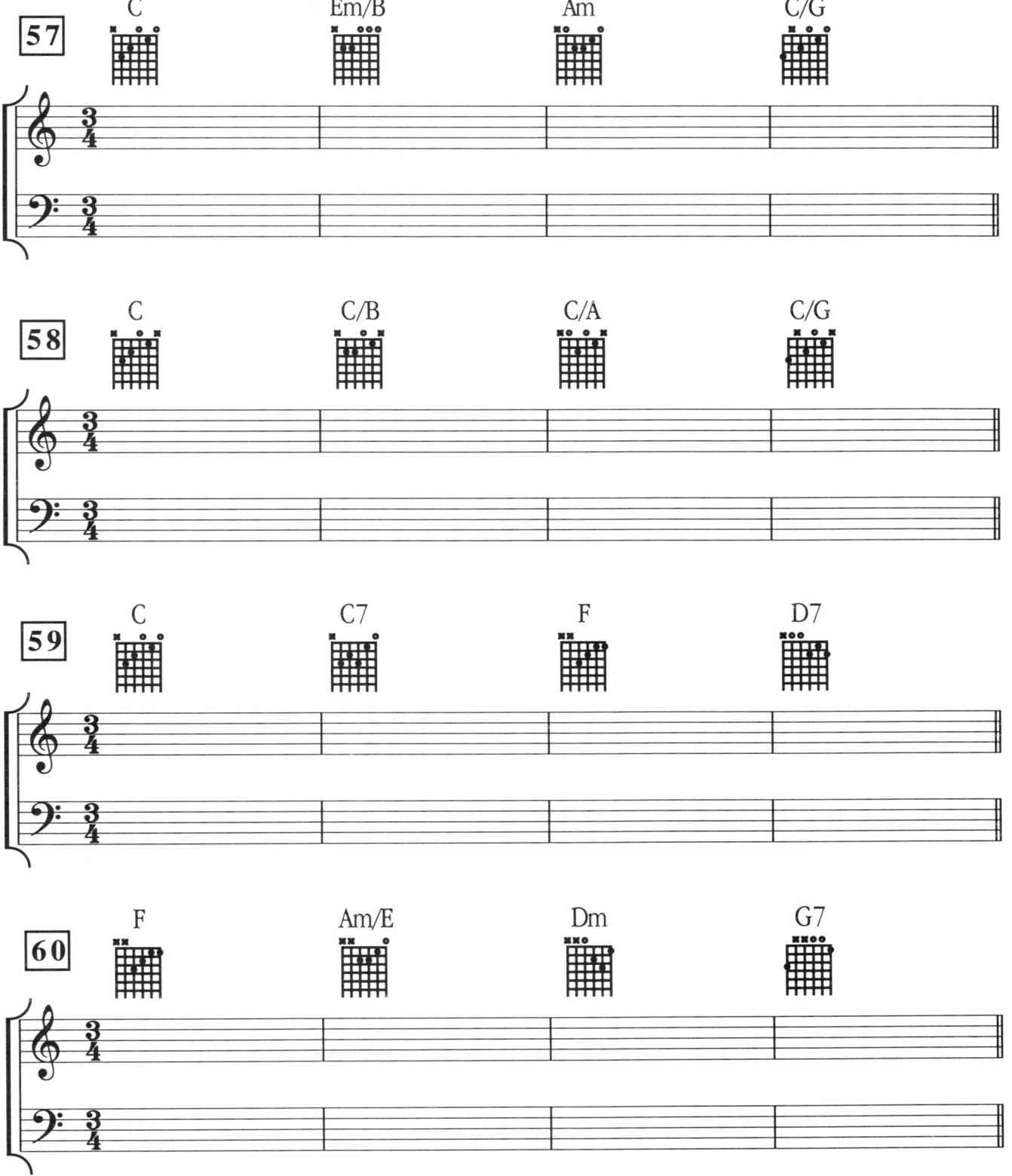

# Eight-Bar Chord Progressions

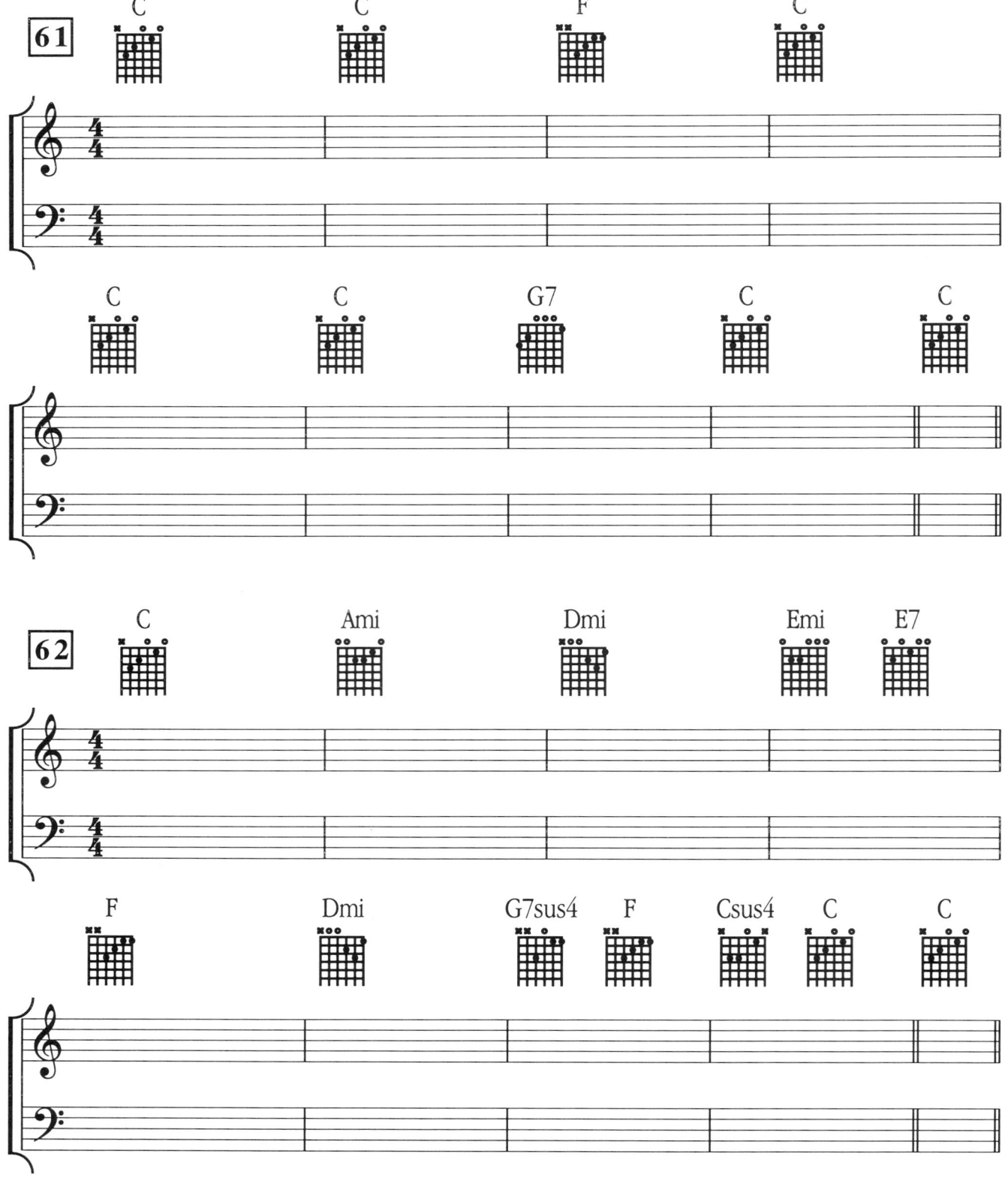

# Eight-Bar Chord Progressions . . . continued

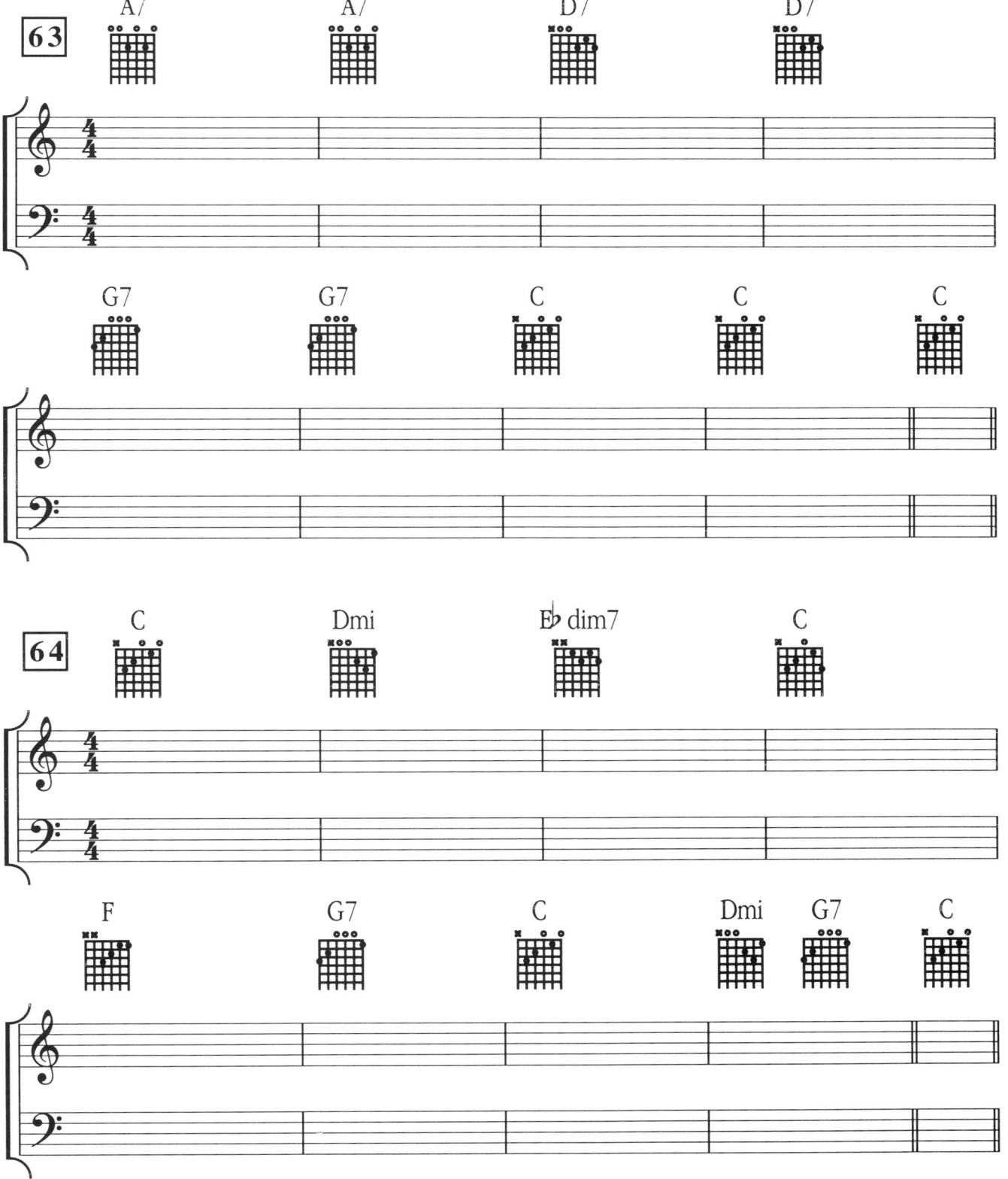

# 16-Bar Chord Progressions

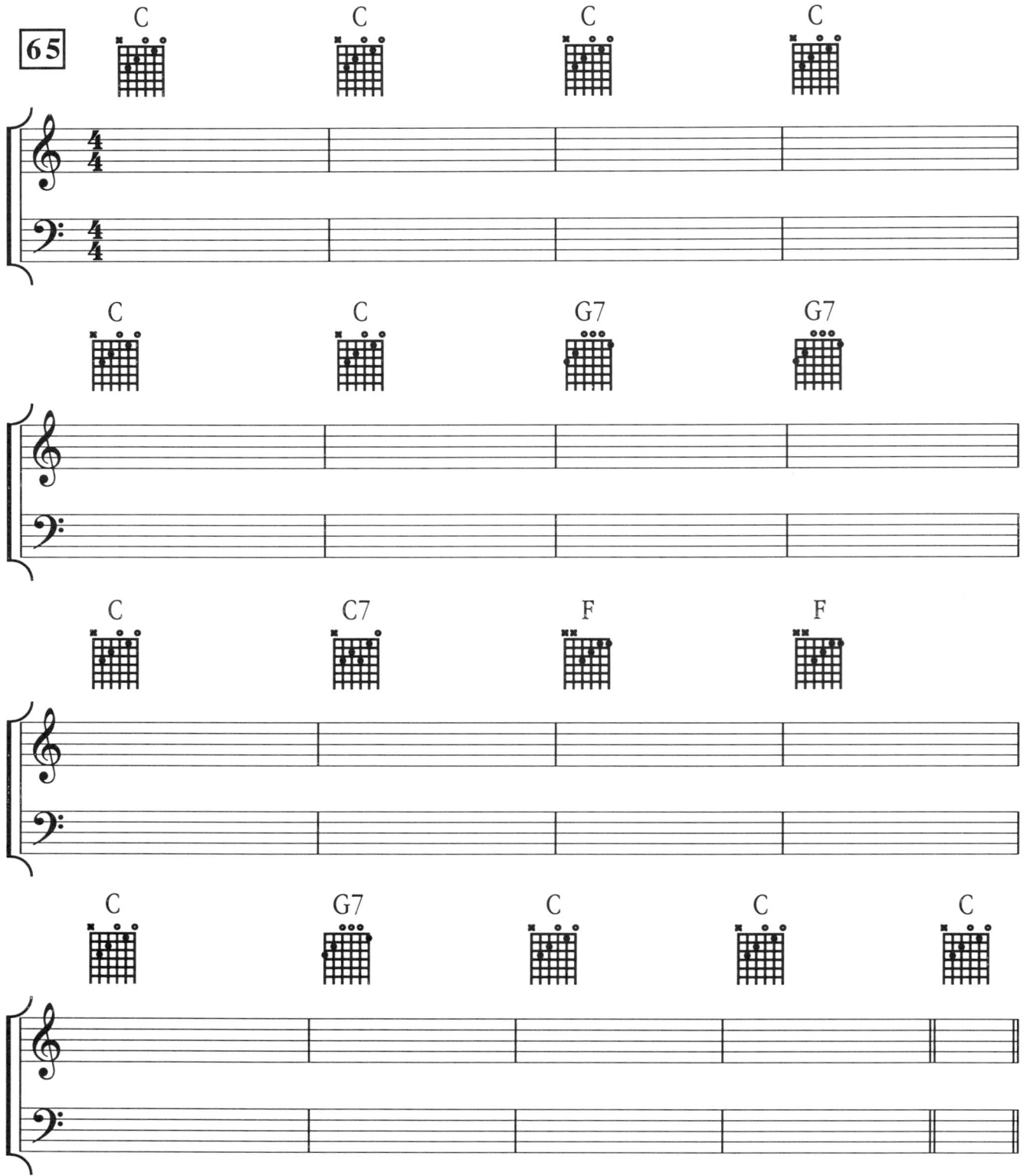

## 16-Bar Chord Progressions . . . continued

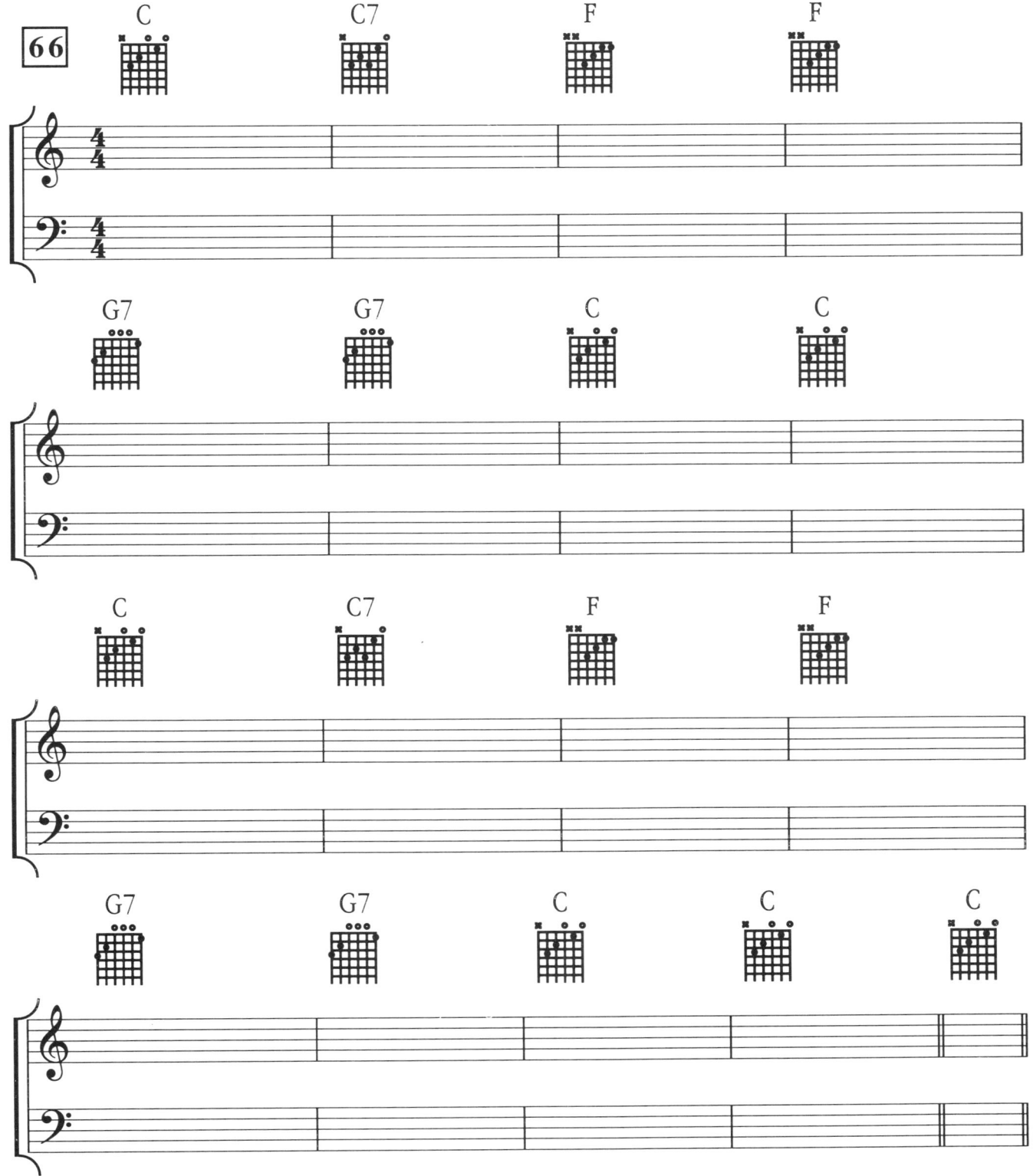

## 16-Bar Chord Progressions . . . continued

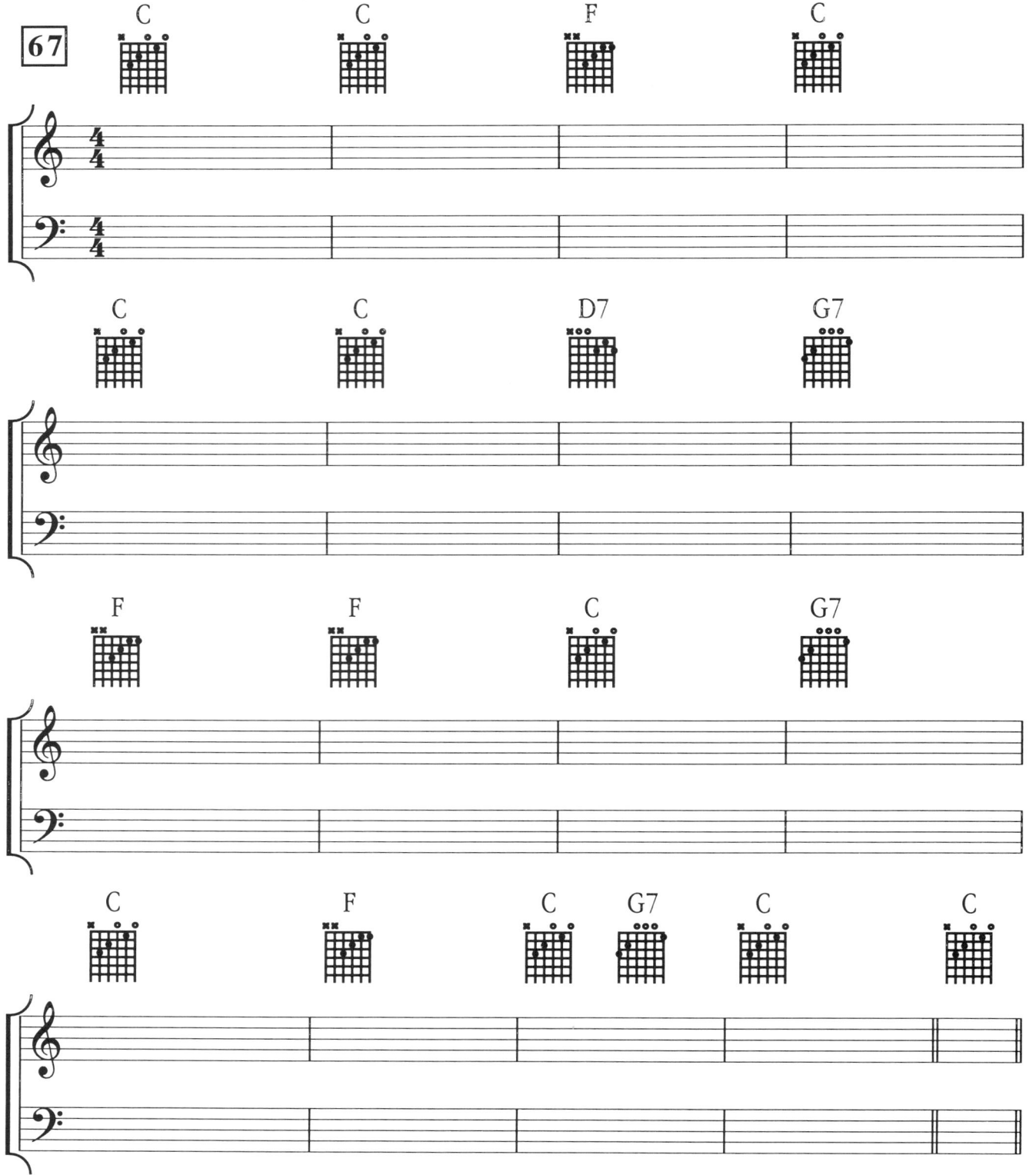

## 16-Bar Chord Progressions . . . continued

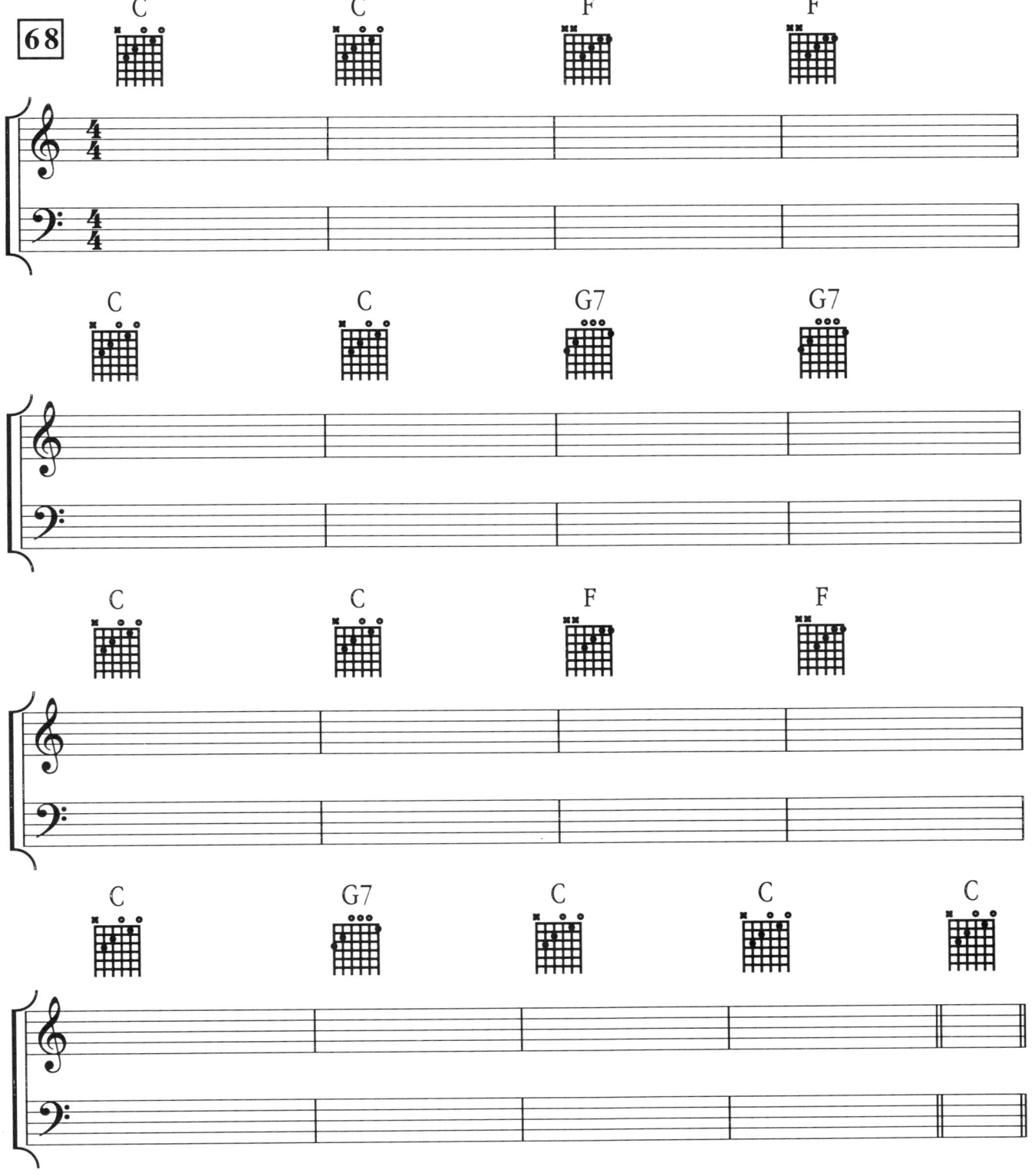

## 16-Bar Chord Progressions . . . continued

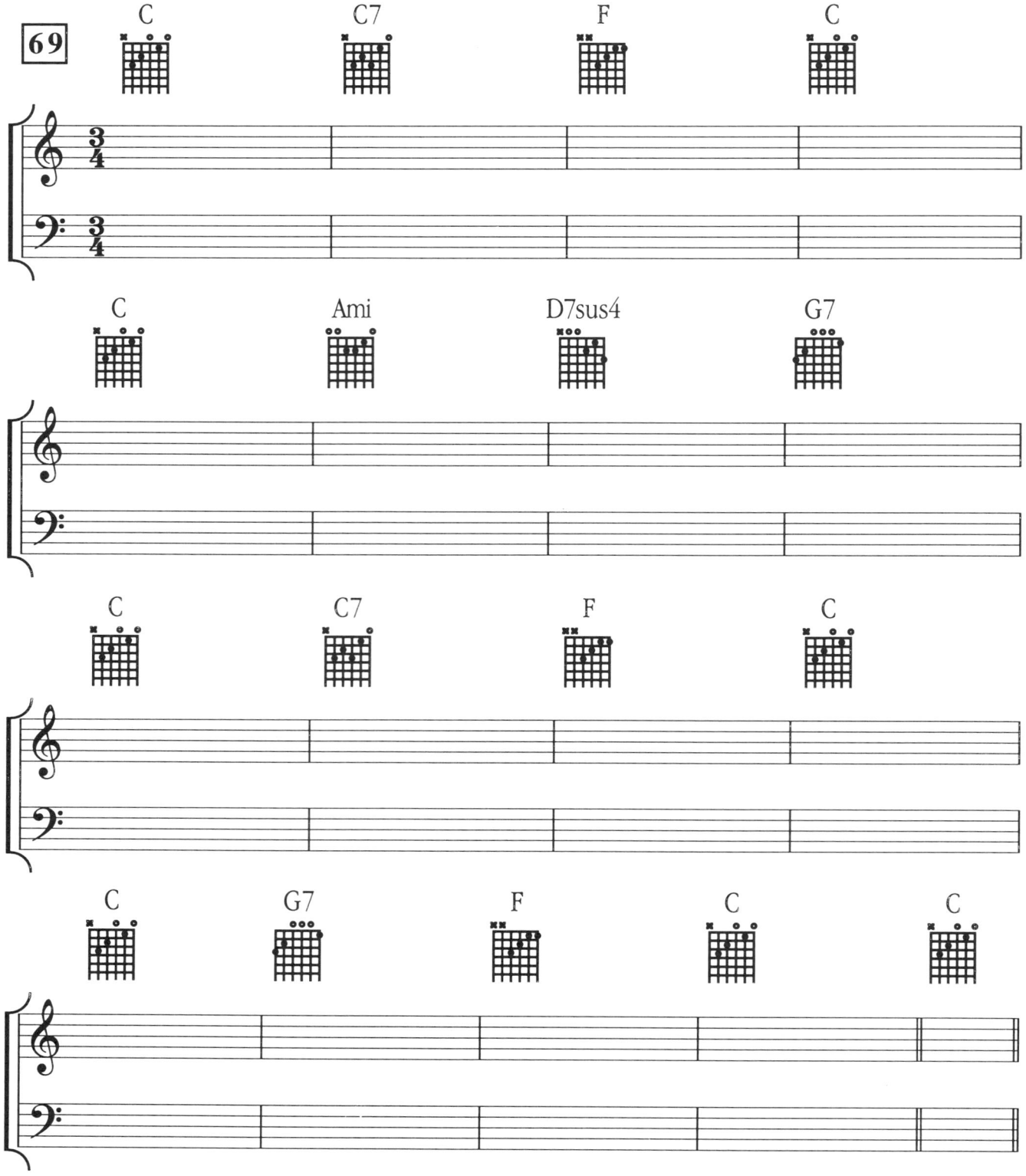

## 16-Bar Verse/Chorus Chord Progressions

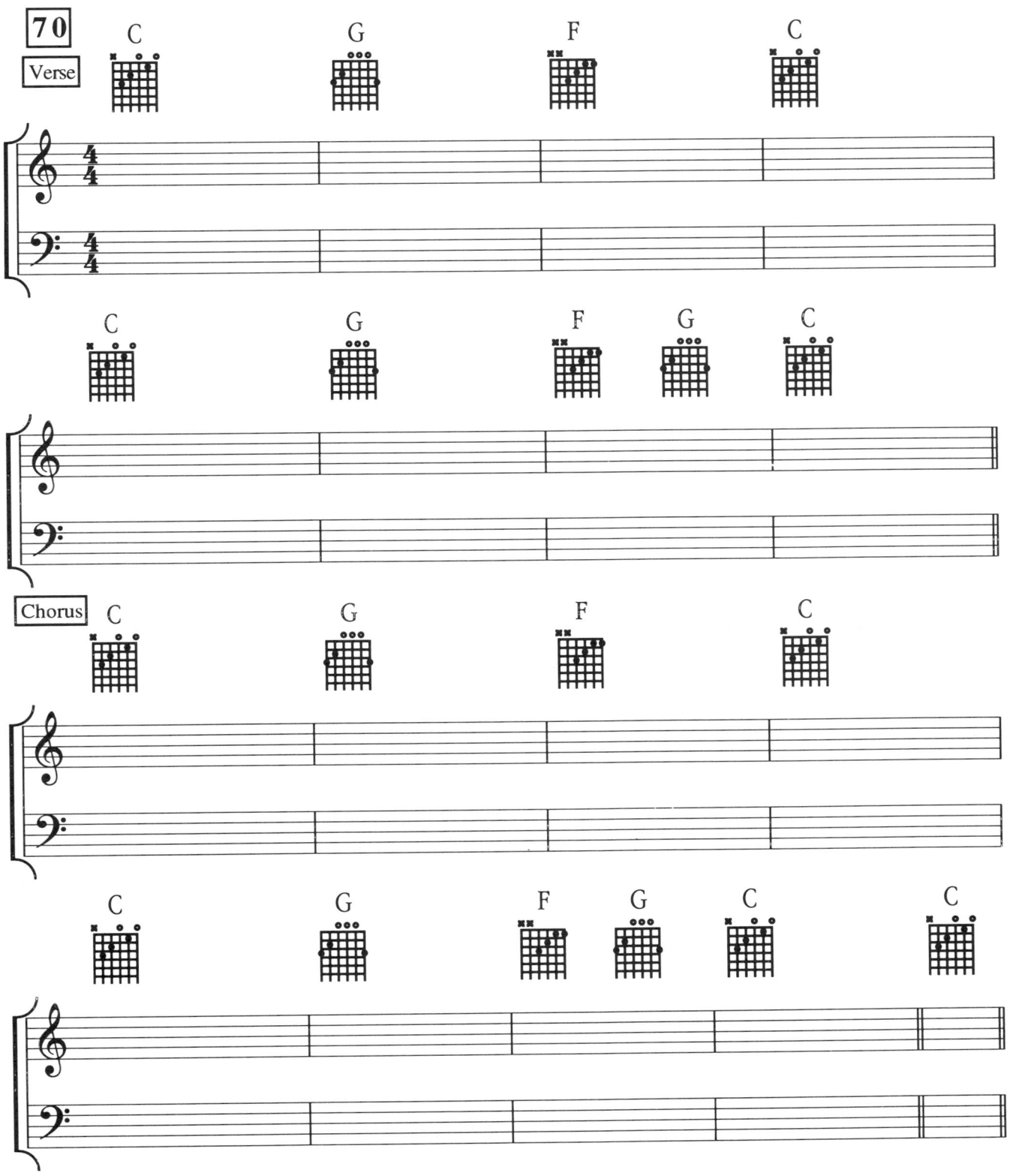

## 16-Bar Verse/Chorus Chord Progressions . . . continued

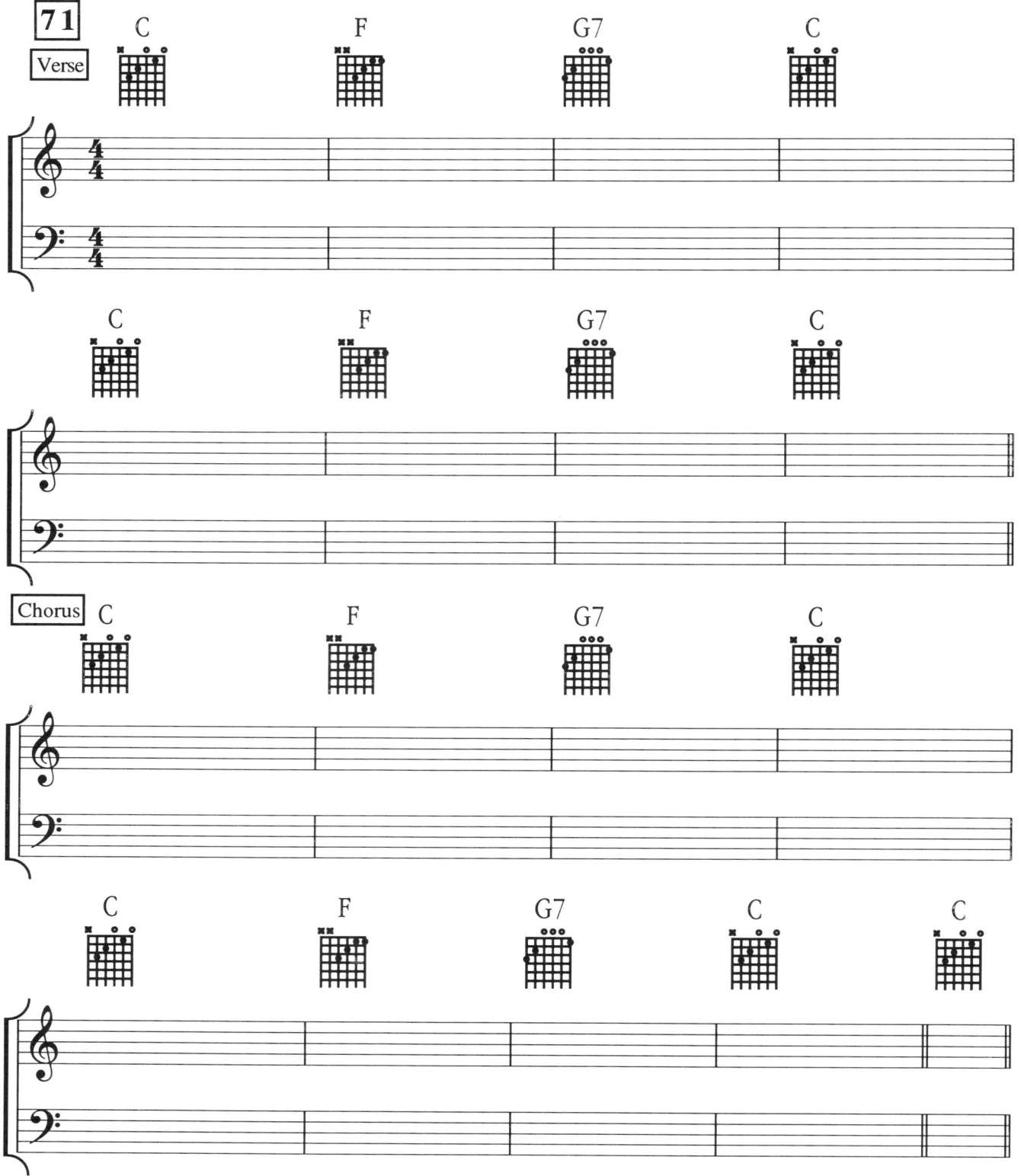

## 16-Bar Verse/Chorus Chord Progressions . . . continued

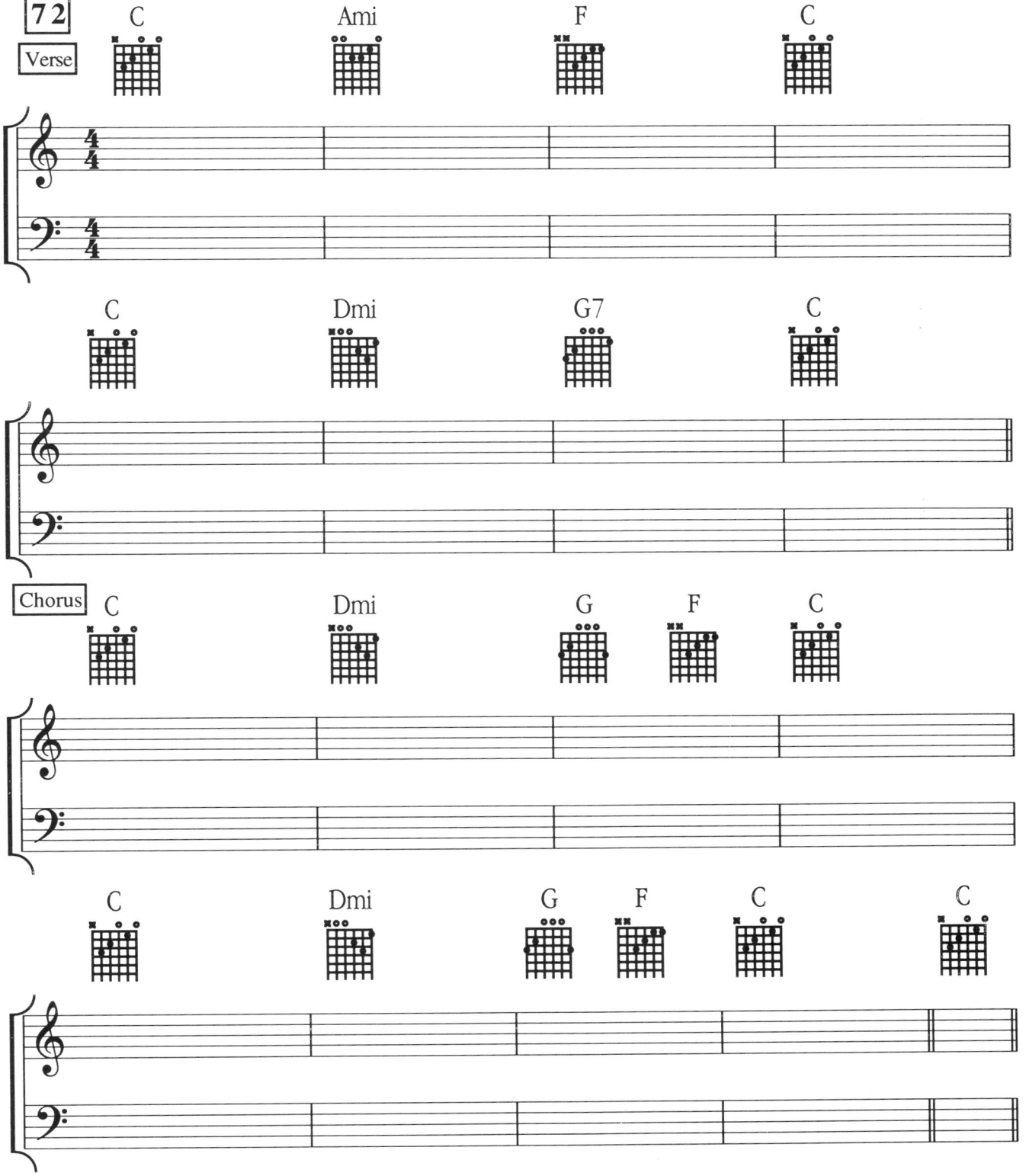

## 16-Bar Verse/Chorus Chord Progressions . . . continued

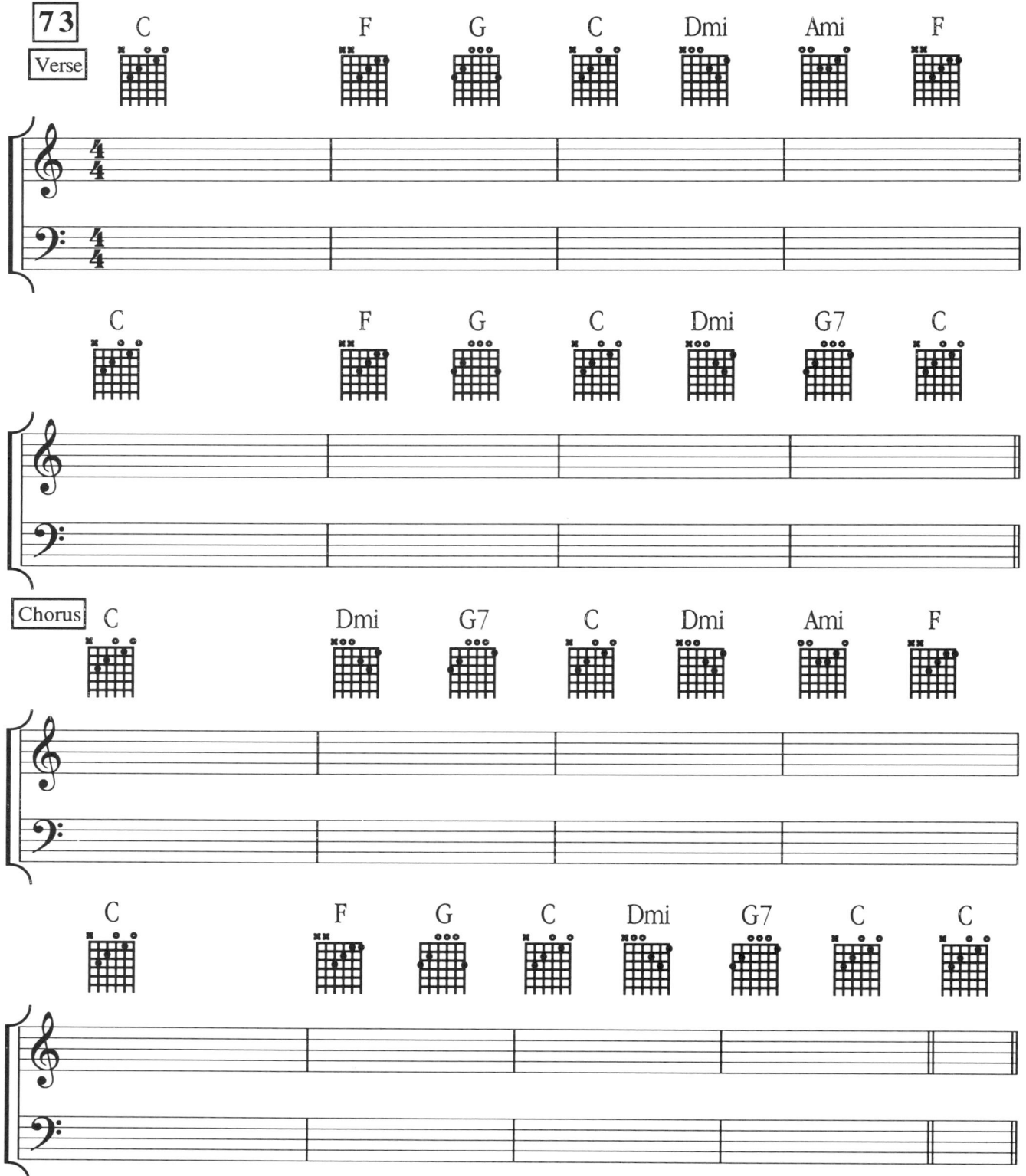

30

## 32-Bar Verse/Chorus Chord Progressions

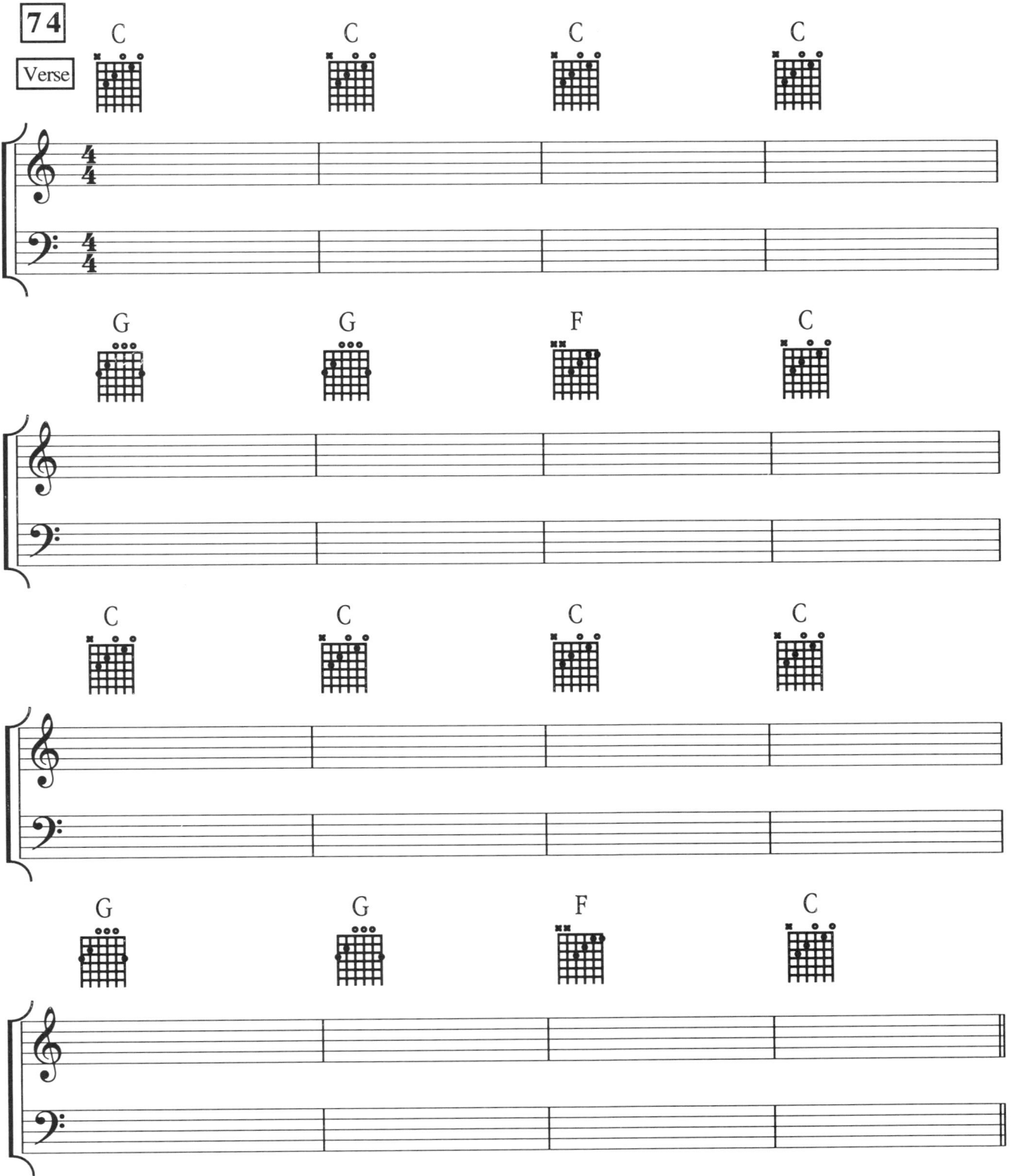

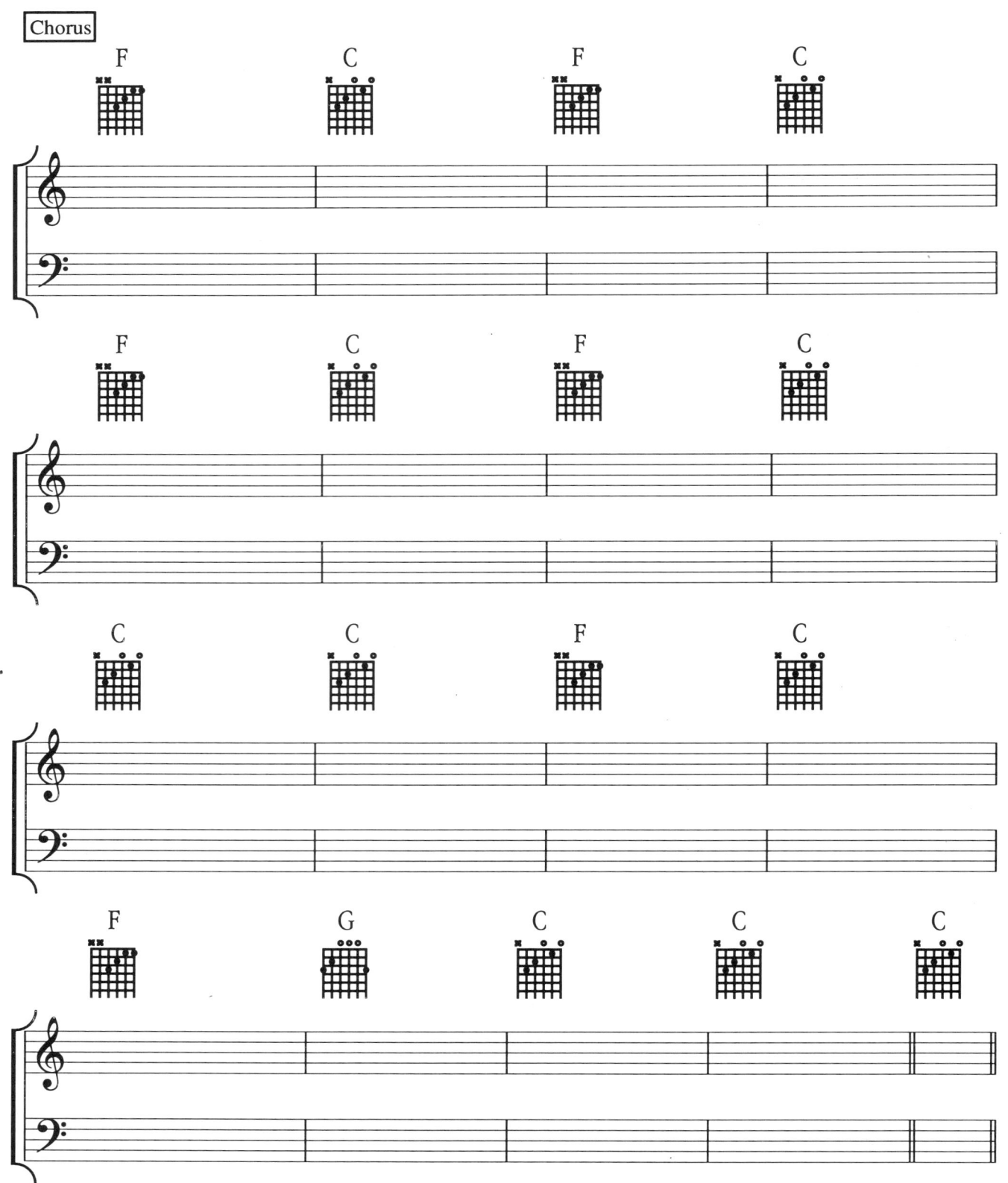

## 32-Bar Verse/Chorus Chord Progressions . . . continued

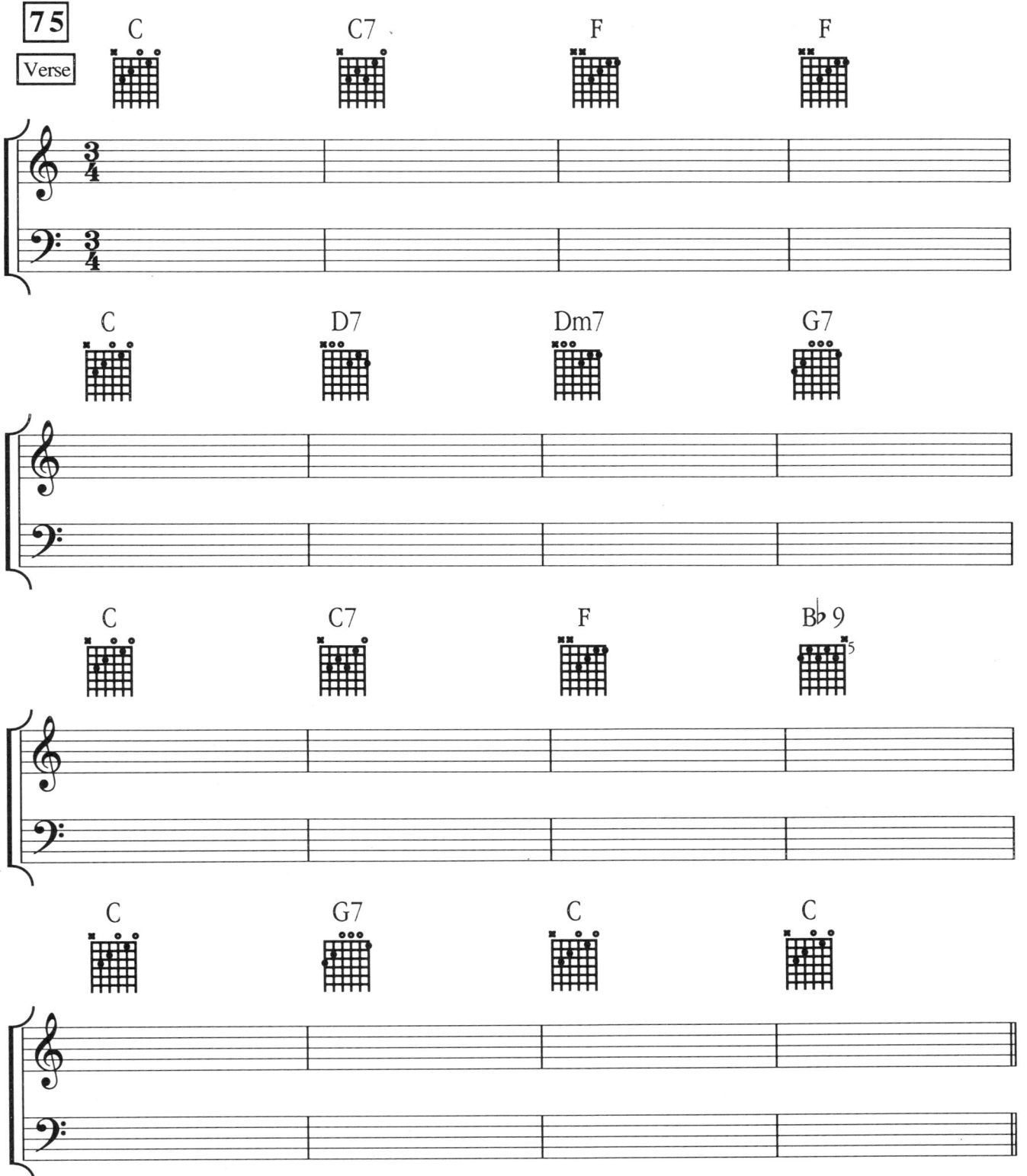

33

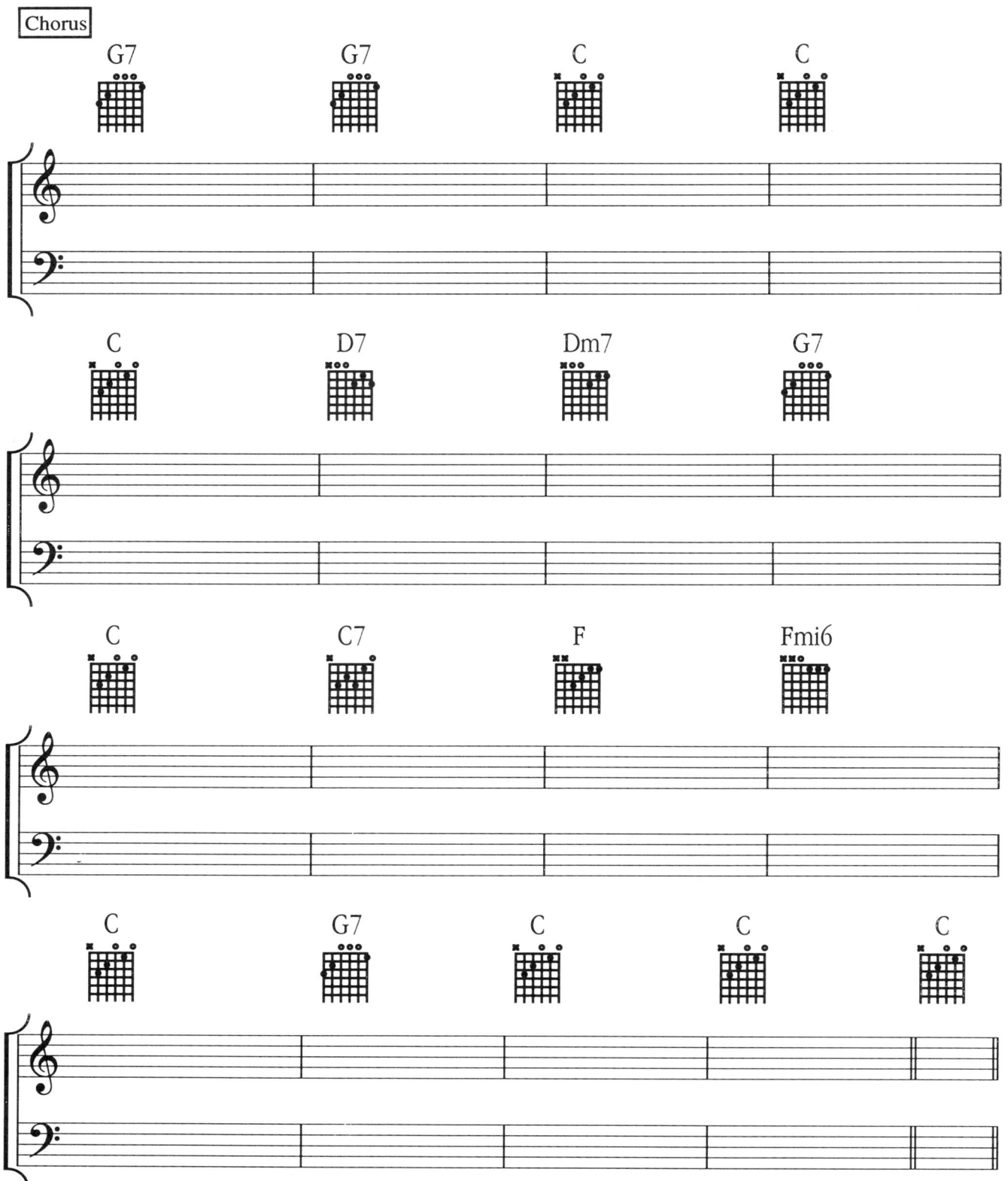

# 12-Bar Blues Progression

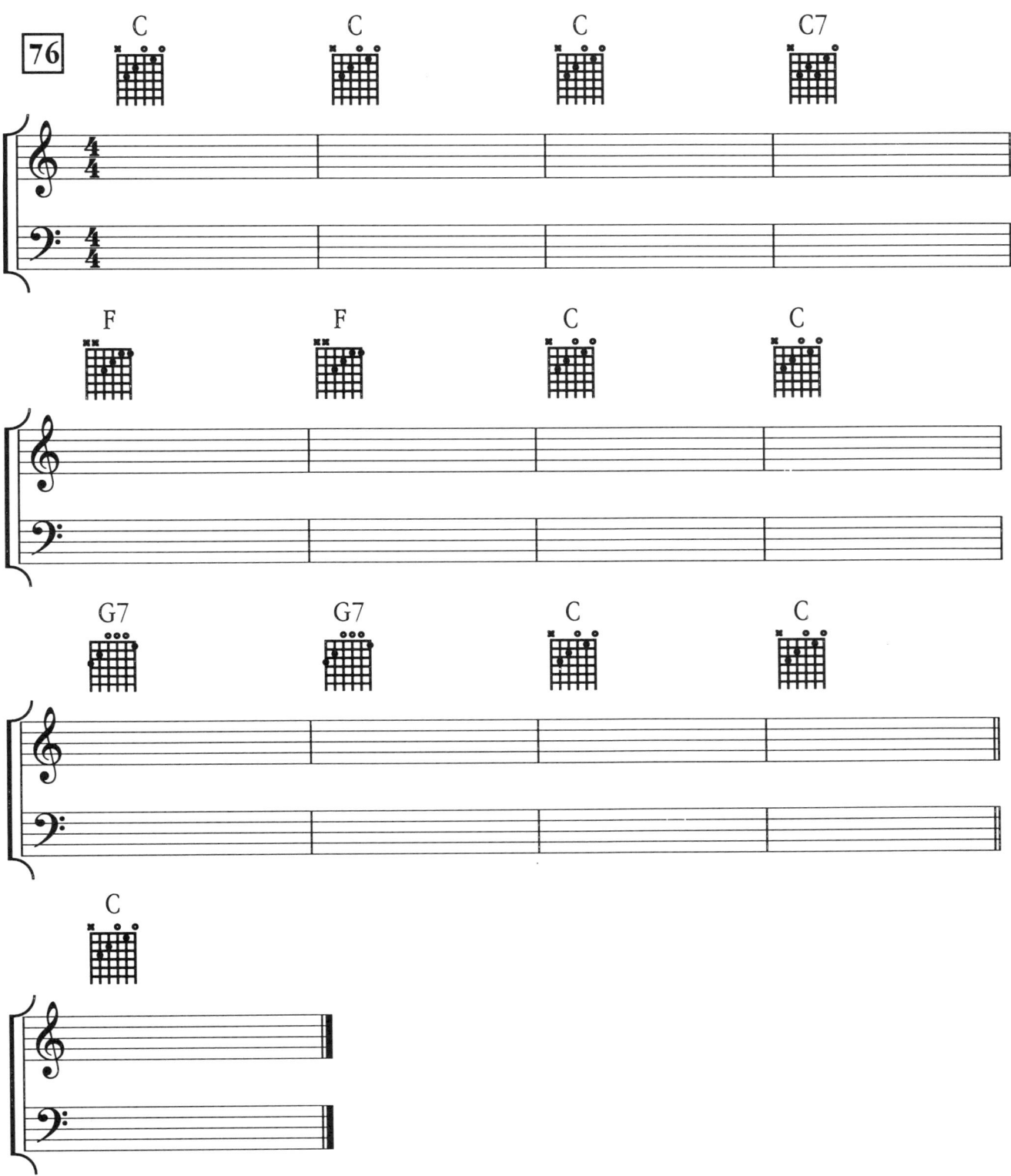

Learn more blues progressions with the following Mel Bay book/CD sets by Larry McCabe:
- **Blues Band Rhythm Guitar**
- **101 Essential Blues Progressions**

# 32-Bar AABA Chord Progressions

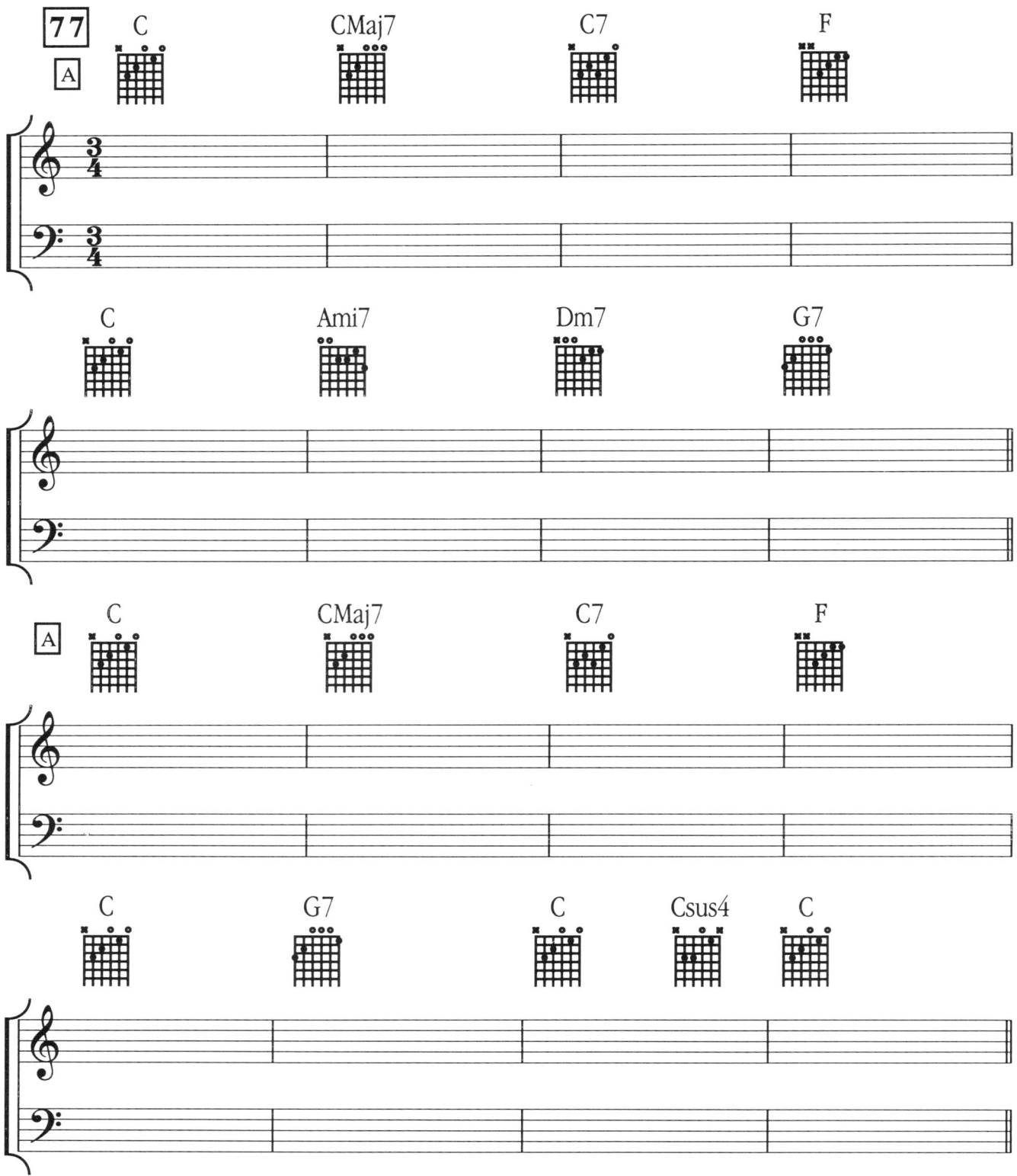

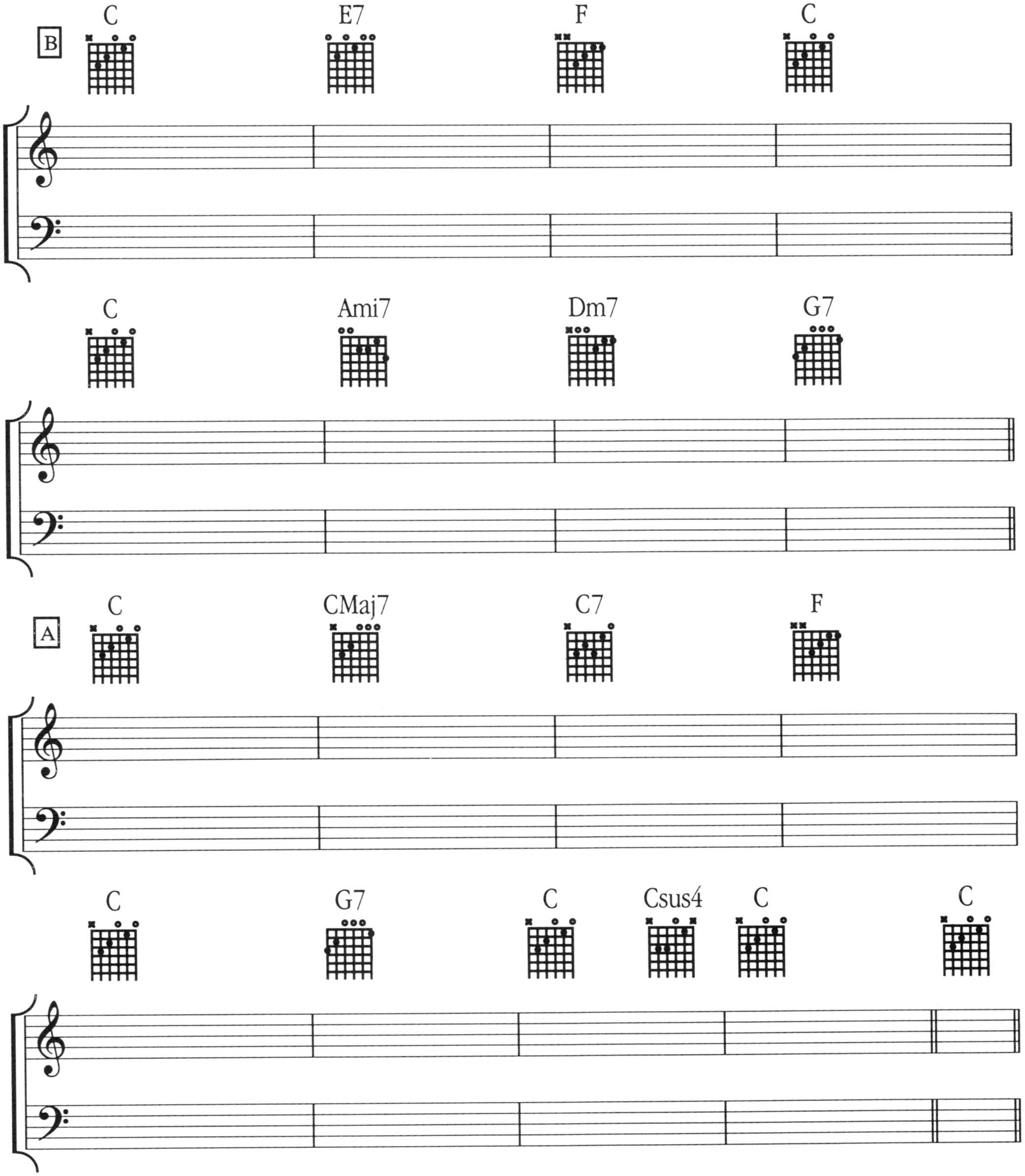
B
C
E7
F
C
C
Ami7
Dm7
G7
A
C
CMaj7
C7
F
C
G7
C
Csus4
C
C

# 32-Bar AABA Chord Progressions . . . continued

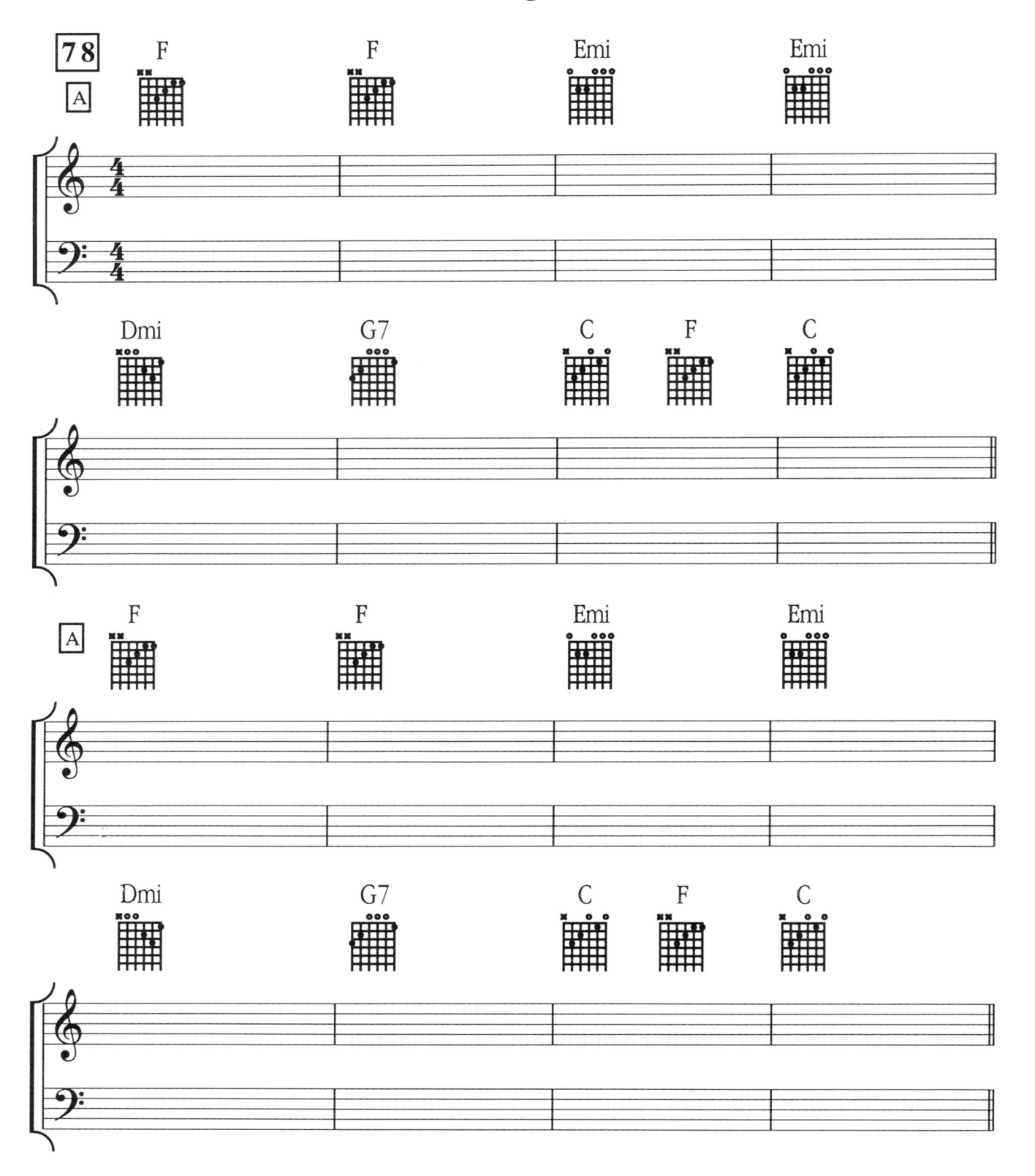

**78**

**A** | F | F | Emi | Emi |
| Dmi | G7 | C  F | C |

**A** | F | F | Emi | Emi |
| Dmi | G7 | C  F | C |

38

| B | F | F | Emi | Emi |

| F | F | D7 | G7 |

| A | F | F | Emi | Emi |

| Dmi | G7 | C | F | C | C |

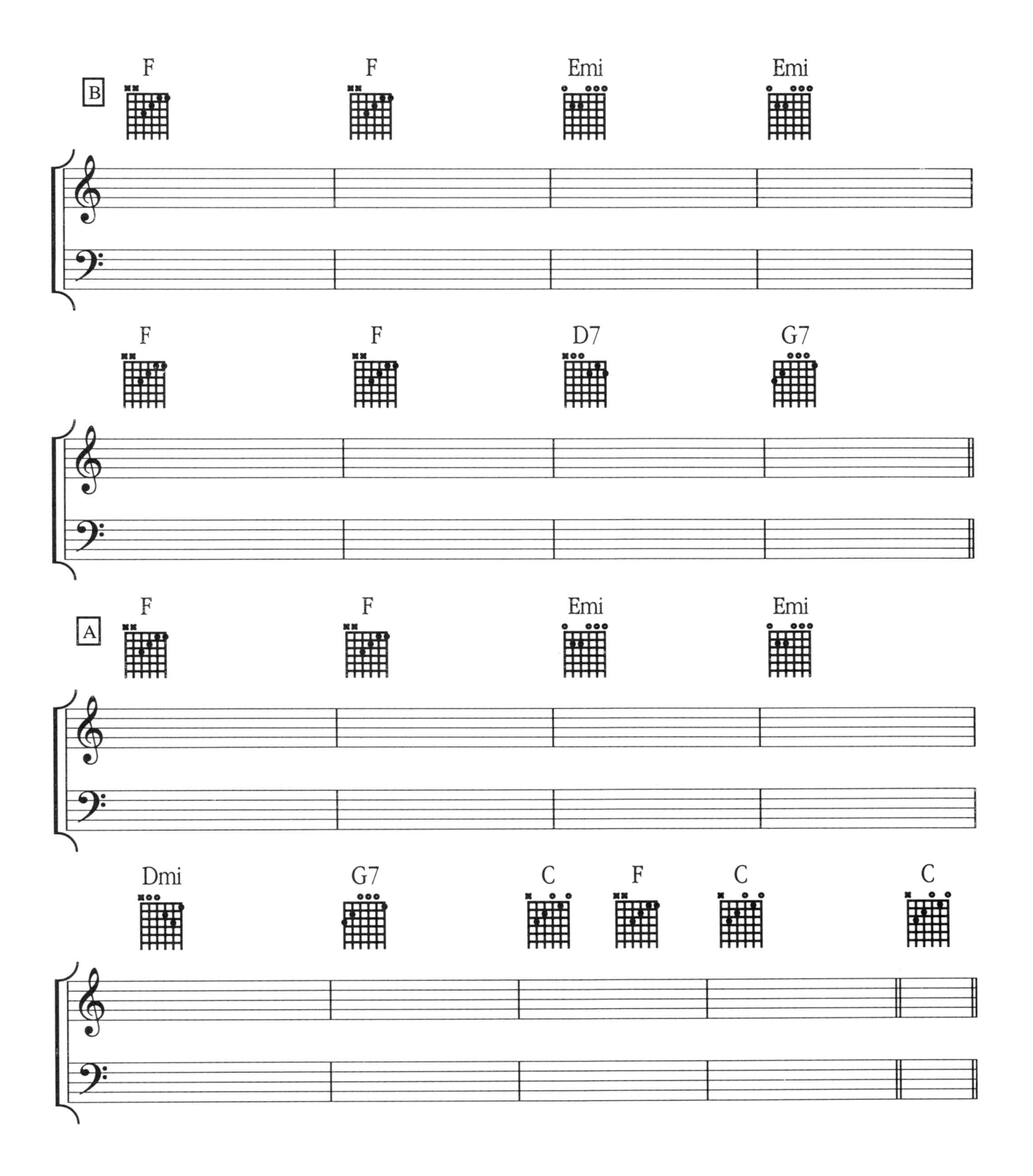

# Bridge Progressions

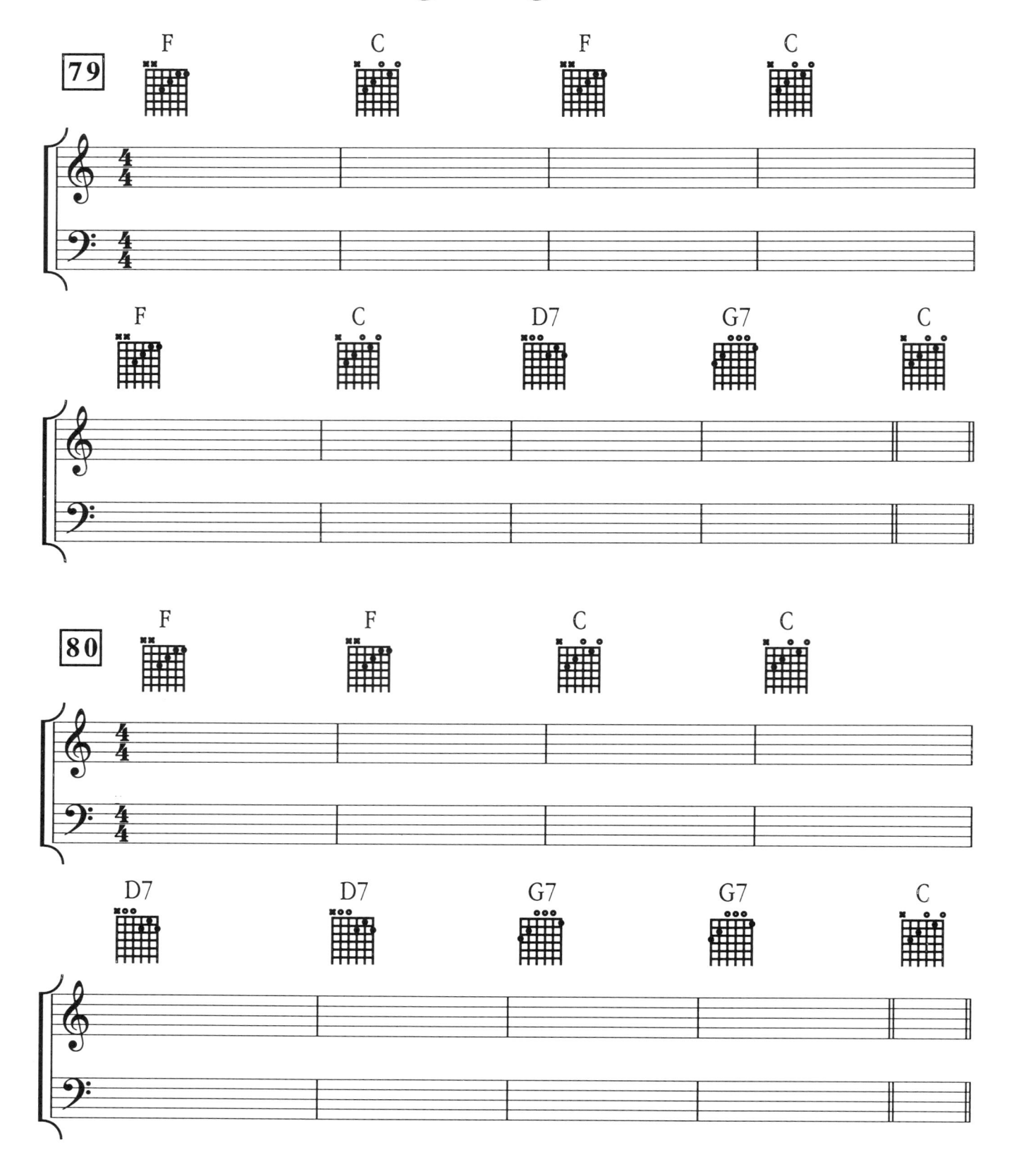

## Bridge Progressions . . . continued

**85** | F | C | G7 | C |
| Emi | A7 | Dmi | G7 | C |

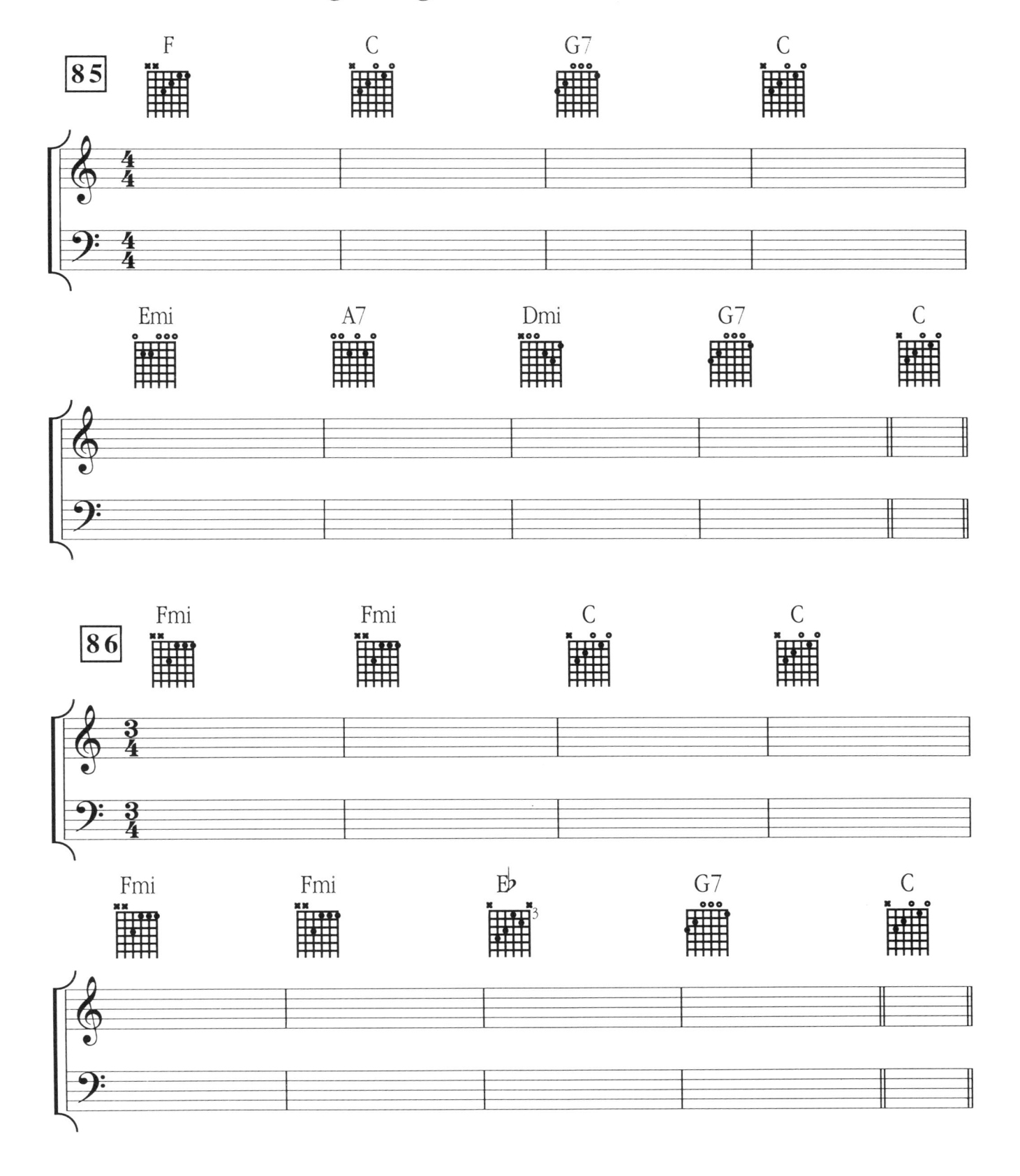

**86** | Fmi | Fmi | C | C |
| Fmi | Fmi | E♭ | G7 | C |

# Bridge Progressions ... continued

**83** | G7 | G7 | C  G7 | C |

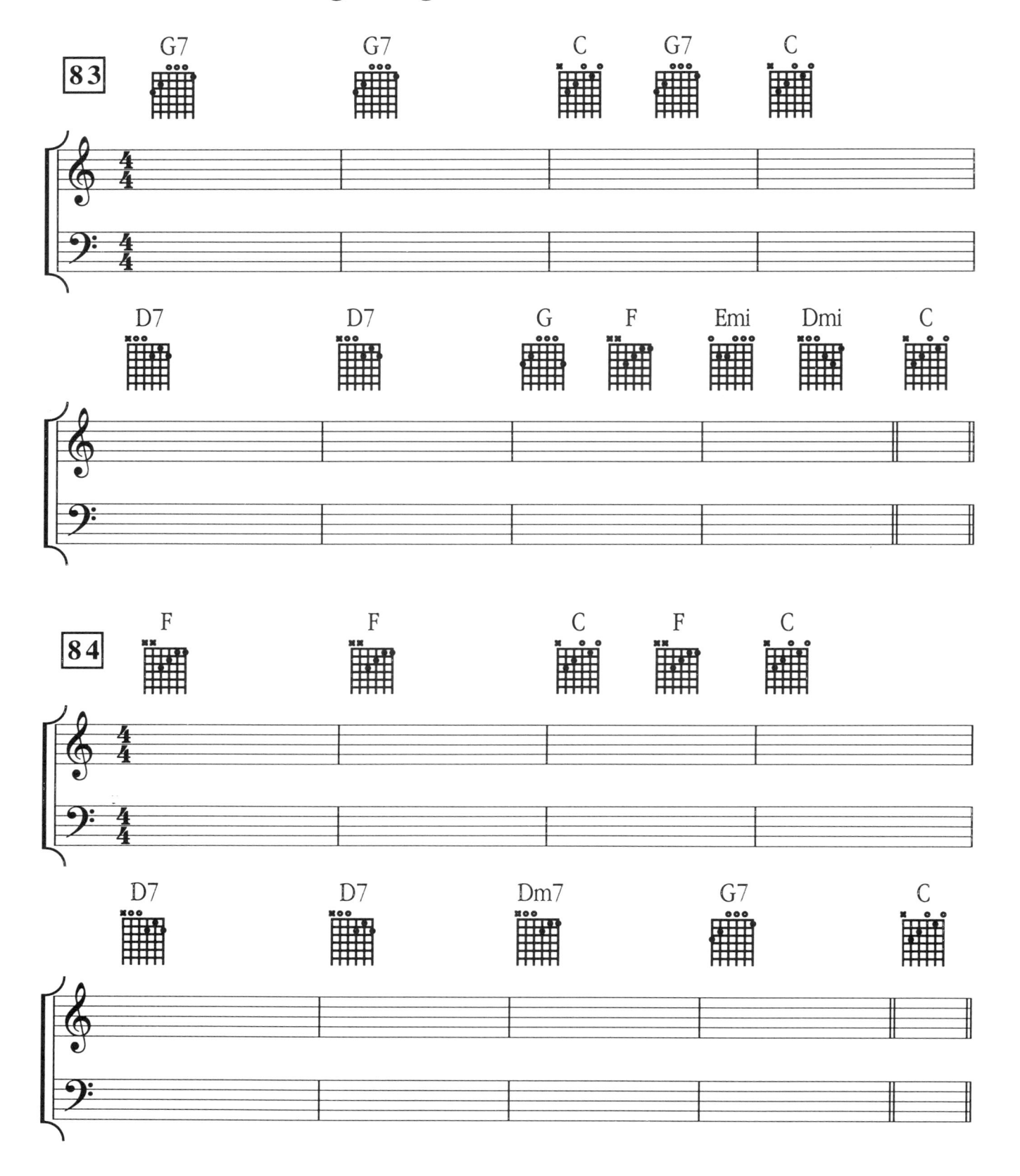

D7 | D7 | G  F | Emi  Dmi | C |

**84** | F | F | C  F | C |

D7 | D7 | Dm7 | G7 | C |

## Bridge Progressions . . . continued

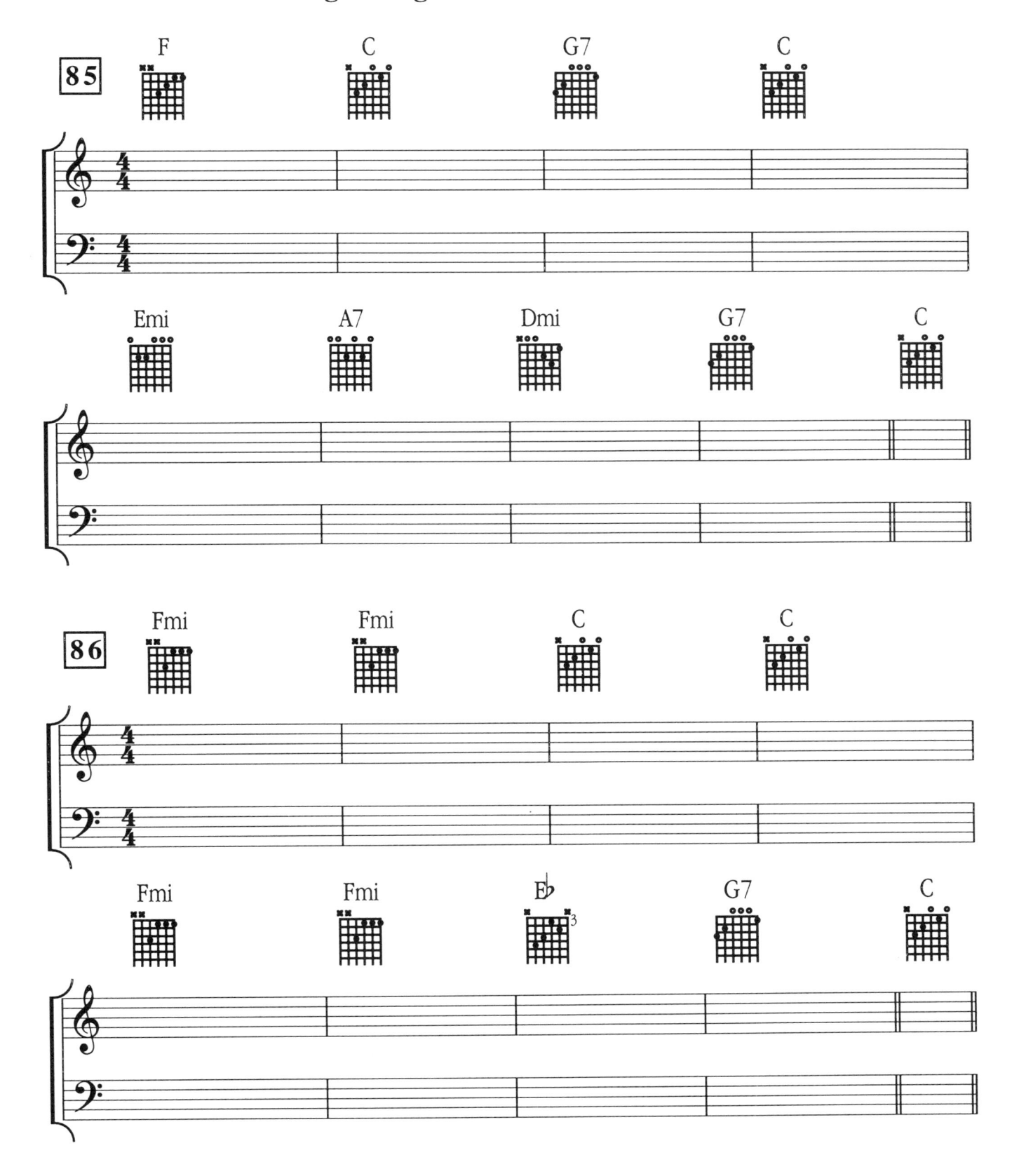

**85** | F | C | G7 | C |
| Emi | A7 | Dmi | G7 | C |

**86** | Fmi | Fmi | C | C |
| Fmi | Fmi | E♭ | G7 | C |

# Turnarounds

A turnaround is a short chord progression (usually two bars) at the end of a section of music.
Each of the following turnarounds resolves to the tonic chord.

**87** | C | Cdim7 | Dm7 | G7 | C |

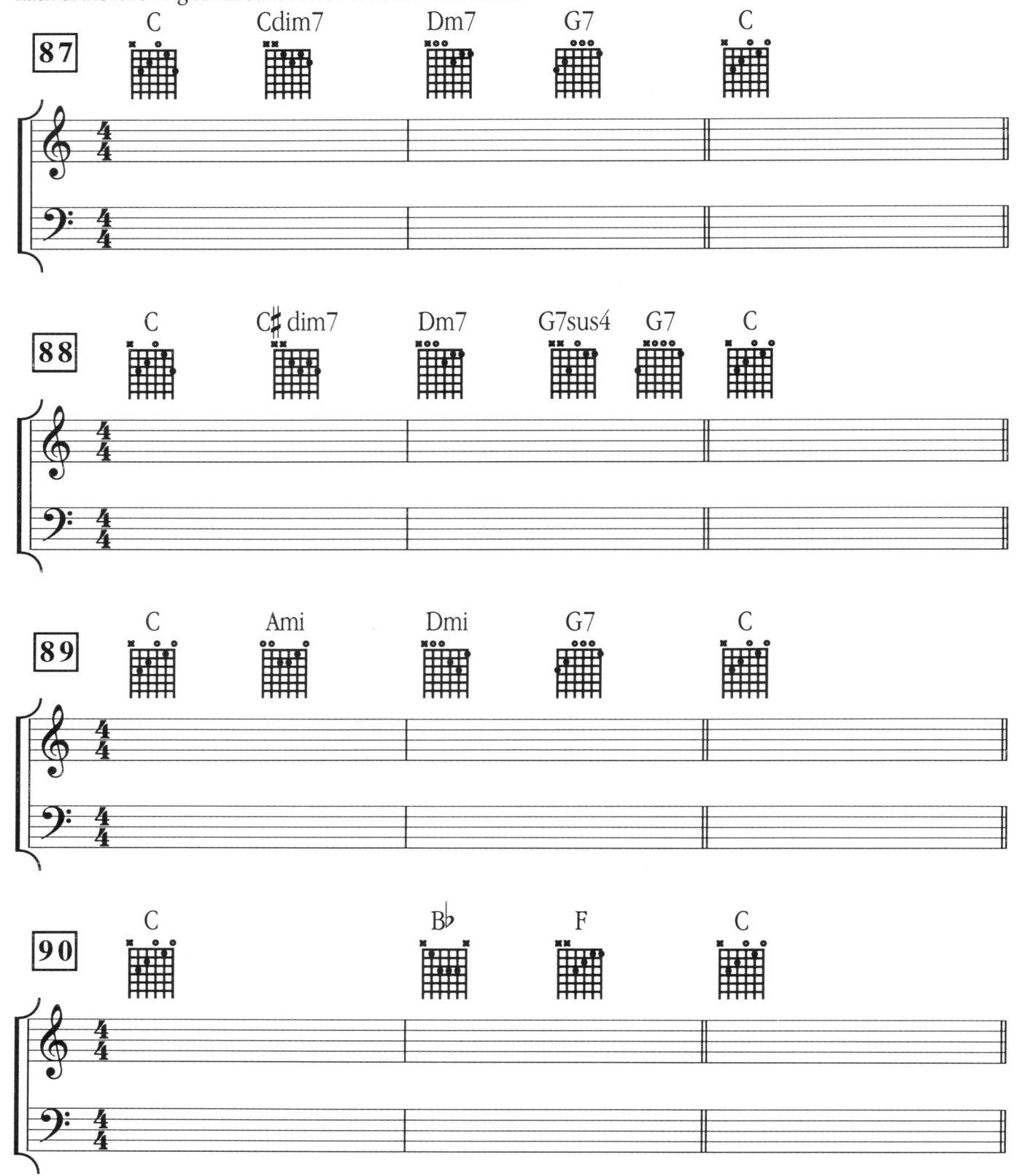

**88** | C | C#dim7 | Dm7 | G7sus4 | G7 | C |

**89** | C | Ami | Dmi | G7 | C |

**90** | C | B♭ | F | C |

# Four-Bar Minor-Key Chord Progressions

**91** | Ami | E7 | Ami | E7 |

**92** | Ami | F | Ami | F |

**93** | Ami | C  D | F | E7 |

**94** | Ami  G | F  E7 | Ami  G | F  E7 |

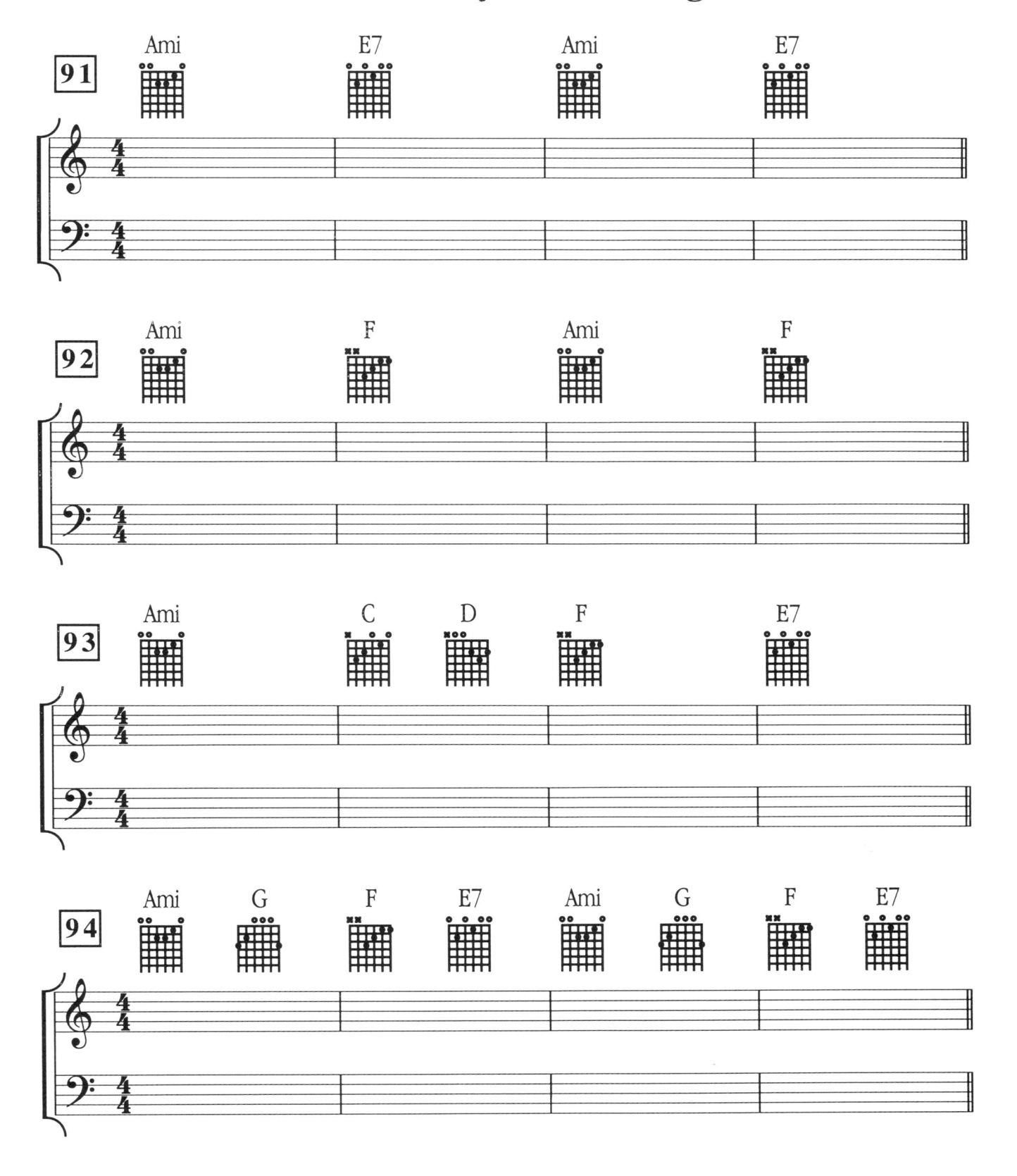

# Four-Bar Minor-Key Chord Progressions . . . continued

**95** | Ami | G | Ami G | Ami

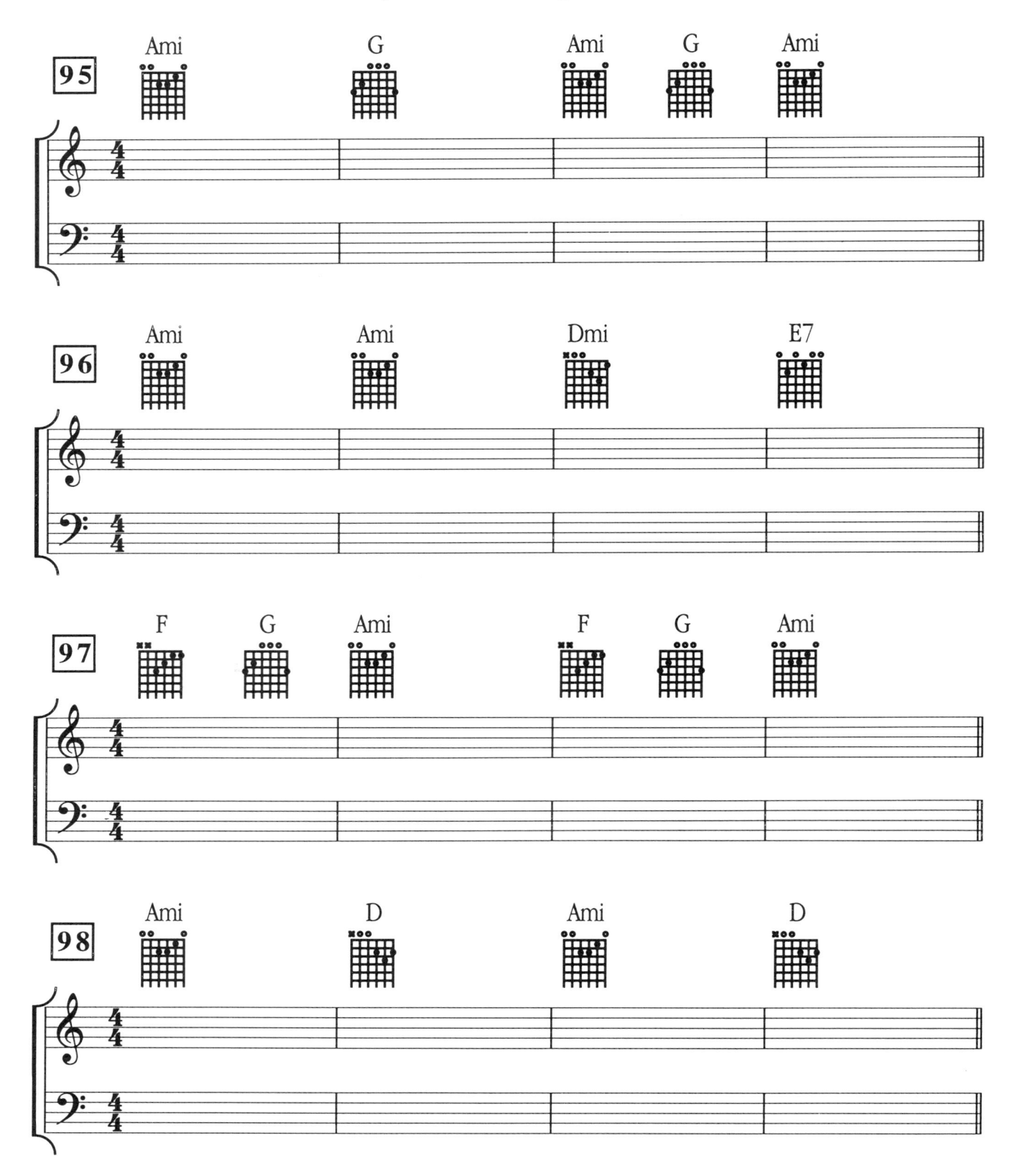

**96** | Ami | Ami | Dmi | E7

**97** | F G Ami | F G Ami

**98** | Ami | D | Ami | D

## Four-Bar Minor-Key Chord Progressions . . . continued

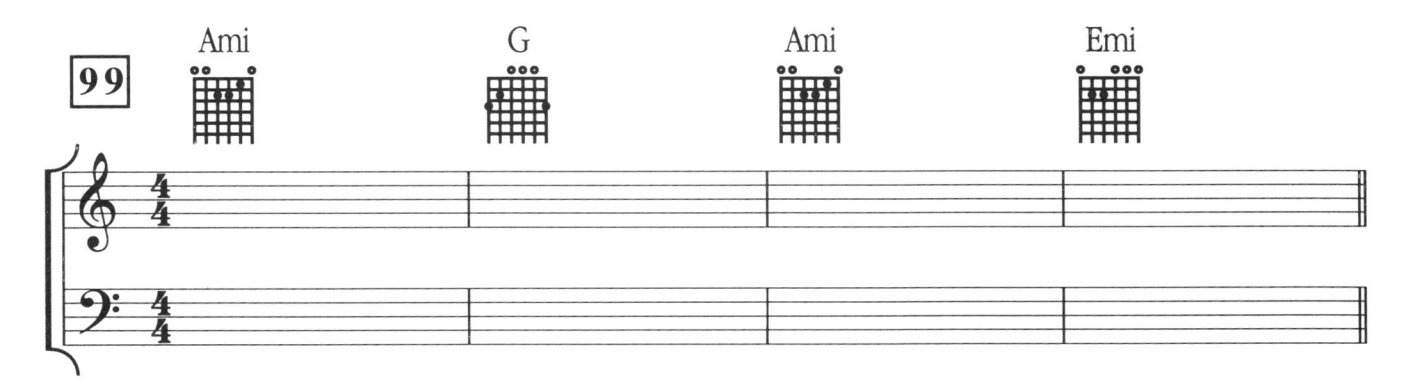

**99** | Ami | G | Ami | Emi |

# Eight-Bar Minor-Key Chord Progressions

**100**

| Ami | E7 | Ami | | Ami | Dmi | Ami | E7 |

| Ami | E7 | Ami | | Ami | E7 | Ami | Ami |

**101**

| Ami | Ami/G♯ | Ami/G | Ami/F♯ |

| FMaj7 | E7 | Ami | F  F  G  Am |

48